Dr. Rainer Twiford, a licensed psychologist, is Coordinator of Children's Services at the Region I Mental Health Center in Clarksdale, Mississippi. Holder of a Ph.D. in Counseling and Educational Psychology, he has published research and presented papers to professional organizations. Dr. Twiford's primary area of interest is child and adolescent behavior.

A CHILD WITH A PROBLEM

A Guide to the Psychological Disorders of Children

Rainer Twiford

A SPECTRUM BOOK

Prentice-Hall, Inc., Englewood Cliffs, New Jersey 07632

Library of Congress Cataloging in Publication Data

Twiford, Rainer, (date)
   A CHILD WITH A PROBLEM

   (A Spectrum Book)
   Bibliography: p.
   Includes index.
   1. Child psychopathology. 2. Child mental
health services. I. Title.
RJ499.T92 1979   618.9'28'9   79-9116
ISBN 0-13-130781-9
ISBN 0-13-130773-8 pbk.

In Loving Memory of Clarence and D.O.

Editorial/production supervision
and interior design by Betty Neville
Cover design by Nancy Kirsh
Manufacturing buyer: Cathie Lenard

PRENTICE-HALL, INTERNATIONAL, INC., *London*
PRENTICE-HALL OF AUSTRALIA, PTY. LIMITED, *Sydney*
PRENTICE-HALL OF CANADA, LTD., *Toronto*
PRENTICE-HALL OF INDIA PRIVATE LIMITED, *New Delhi*
PRENTICE-HALL OF JAPAN, INC., *Tokyo*
PRENTICE-HALL OF SOUTHEAST ASIA PTE. LTD., *Singapore*
WHITEHALL BOOKS LIMITED, *Wellington, New Zealand*

CONTENTS

Contents

PREFACE

This book is an attempt to describe the nature of childhood
psychological disorders clearly and concisely to parents and
teachers. I have observed a widespread lack of knowledge
among teachers and parents regarding behavioral and emotional problems of children. It is all too common to witness
responsible, informed adults using archaic and mystical
approaches in their explanations of atypical child behavior. A
primary purpose of this book is to discourage the use of over-
worked and misleading diagnostic labels. Also, I hope to provide teachers and parents with some idea of what they may
realistically expect of children who carry valid psychological
diagnoses.

As every teacher knows, there are a vast number of
children whose academic and social functioning is, for one
reason or another, impaired. I have seen teachers express
agonizing frustration in their attempts to understand and cope

with the so-called atypical child. This book will aid teachers and parents in recognizing, treating, and understanding the major psychological disorders afflicting children. The most current information available is provided in readable and cogent form. I have purposefully attempted to avoid complex professional jargon and endless citations of research studies and authors.

It is necessary to point out that the scientific study of child behavior is a relatively new endeavor and that information is often sparse and inconclusive. The parent and teacher should be keenly aware of the limits of current knowledge. This will enable the responsible adult to discount hasty, invalid diagnoses and to develop a healthy skepticism toward psychological classification in general.

I have attempted to shed light on some of the unique problems of the developing child. It is my hope that the reader will approach these problems of childhood with a heightened degree of sophistication and understanding. To fight public ignorance in this area is to enhance the potential of countless children who are burdened with psychological disorders.

ACKNOWLEDGMENTS

There are many people who are responsible for making this book a reality. I would like to thank Peter Carson, Ph.D. and Cecilia Marshall, M.S.S.W. for their extremely helpful suggestions. My gratitude to Lynne Lumsden, Senior Editor of Spectrum Books, and her assistant, Frank Moorman, for their competent guidance. I thank David Lail, J.D. for his skillful editorial assistance. Joseph C. Battaile, M.D. and Van Burnham, M.D. also supplied helpful information. My sincere appreciation to Ann Bolm for her accurate and tremendously speedy preparation of the manuscript. Finally, I wish to acknowledge my wife, Marsha, for her continuing love and support.

Chapter 1

INTRODUCTION TO THE NATURE OF PSYCHOLOGICAL DISORDERS

DEFINITION

The term *psychological disorder* generally means any behavior or set of behaviors that interferes with a child's normal growth and development. Usually a poor quality of behavior is observed in one or more of the following areas: (1) intellectual and academic performance, (2) emotional adjustment, and (3) social functioning. Although all children show temporary setbacks and minor adjustment problems throughout the growth process, children with psychological disorders usually display distinctly inadequate or self-defeating behavior patterns. Several of these disorders are detectable by psychological tests (e.g., mental retardation, phobic reactions) or through the clinical interview process (e.g., hyperactivity, brain dysfunction). However, psychological diagnosis is, in some instances, nebulous and arbitrary, and the science of psychological classification is not infallible. Therefore, the parent or teacher should approach the use of diagnostic labels cautiously.

LABELING

Many parents and teachers freely apply such fashionable terms as hyperactive, dyslexic, emotionally disturbed, overanxious, and the like to the behavior of children. These are but a few of the myriad available labels that can be detrimental to a child's development.

Research has documented that the use of labels often contributes to the development of poor self-esteem in children. A child's knowledge of his or her label may serve to create feelings of insecurity, rejection, and hostility. Frequently, labels tend to be self-fulfilling in that children learn to behave in a manner dictated by the label. For example, it has been demonstrated that children who are told that they are "bright" tend to perform better academically than a matched control group that was labeled "average."

Furthermore, children are frequently mislabeled by parents, teachers, and professionals. Children grow and develop so rapidly that reliable diagnoses may be only temporarily appropriate. For example, a child may be labeled *hyperactive* as a result of behavior observed during a transient situational crisis, such as the death of a parent. This label will tend to follow the child after the hyperactive behavior has diminished. One possible result could be the unnecessary administration of psychoactive drugs prescribed at one time for a condition that no longer exists.

Parents and teachers may also be too hasty in suggesting labels for children. Behavioral labels can serve as vehicles for the transfer of blame for unacceptable behavior from the adult to the child. The adult is thus equipped with a handy excuse for the child's misbehavior, and he or she is reluctant to accept responsibility for changing the behavior. The goal of altering the undesirable behavior is blocked by the adult's misperception that the problem is inherent in the child rather than in the environment provided by the adult.

It should be noted that psychological diagnosis and classification is extremely useful when properly applied by qualified professionals. The use of labels among professionals enables communication to be clear and efficient. One word may represent several symptoms or behaviors that the child is currently demonstrating. A detailed description of the child's behavior and the circumstances that elicit the behavior will assist the professional in establishing a diagnosis and treatment plan for the child. Even then, the diagnostic label should be used with restraint and should not replace more comprehensive behavioral descriptions.

PERSPECTIVES IN CONFLICT

In order to enhance the reader's knowledge of the nature of psychological disorders, the predominant concepts (models) of psychological disorder need to be presented. Two of the major concepts of abnormal behavior are the medical model and the learning perspective. Models are metaphors that help us select, represent, and organize events in a meaningful manner. Although these models are inadequate representations, they serve as interpretive guides to abnormal behavior so that the behavior makes sense to us. The model that we learn will determine the way in which we view and cope with abnormal child behavior.

The *medical model* of abnormal behavior holds that psychological disorders constitute an illness or disease. Some authors contend that a disease is any significant deviation from normal standards whereby adequate functioning is impaired. It is not important whether or not physical, mental, or behavioral functioning is involved. The medical model perpetuates the use of such terms as syndrome, symptom, prognosis, and cure. Additionally, those who adhere to the medical model will tend to seek medical professionals (e.g., physicians and nurses) in the treatment of abnormal behavior.

Alternatively, proponents of the *learning model* maintain that all behavior, normal or abnormal, is the result of learning. Physiological conditions, such as brain damage or genetic defects, serve only to limit the range of learning. Learning is determined by the specific nature of the interaction between the organism and its environment. This set of assumptions creates an approach to child behavior that is disparate with the medical model. Techniques of behavior change largely rely on conditioning procedures rather than administration of medication. Parents, teachers, and others who are responsible for the child's development are usually involved in the treatment process. The treatment of abnormal behavior most likely involves psychologists with special training in the area of learning principles.

Again, a model is an inadequate representation of reality. Therefore, it is advisable to study the strengths and to recognize the weaknesses of each perspective. This orientation is referred to as *eclecticism*. It is safe to say that most, but not all, effective general practitioners in the area of general childhood behavior disorders are eclectic. Those professionals who are highly specialized usually tend to be more "pure" in their adherence to a specific perspective.

Chapter 2

BIZARRE BEHAVIOR: INFANTILE AUTISM AND SCHIZOPHRENIA

INFANTILE AUTISM

Many parents provide histories to physicians and child behavior experts similar to the following:

> *I began noticing that Chris was different within the first few months of life. He was something of a fussy baby and didn't respond very well to people. He always rejected affection, particularly in the form of physical contact. He would rarely look at anyone and didn't seem to recognize family members. Now, he is unable to express himself verbally, and he often repeats words and phrases that he hears. He often copies simple actions of others and uses these in most new situations. He is performing very poorly in his preschool class because of his lack of social interest and his inability to communicate with others. I have noticed his increasing tendency to scratch his arms to the point*

5

that bleeding occurs and scabs develop. He just sits alone and
scratches for hours. He is preoccupied with unusual things,
such as the knob on the broken dishwasher in the garage.

This is a description of some of the behaviors typically observed
in children who are diagnosed as *autistic*.
Infantile autism is a devastating disorder that occurs in an
estimated 2 to 4 children per 10,000. There are 2½ to 3 boys
for every girl with this disorder. This condition is usually
detectable during the first two years of life.

Autistic children show an aloofness characterized by a
total lack of social interest. Many autistic children actively
avoid eye contact and physical closeness to others. The infant
vigorously resists the parents' attempts at cuddling and affection. Most autistic children adjust poorly to changes in their
environments. Simple, repetitive responses are displayed in a
variety of situations. For example, Chris was often observed
tugging his ear and saying to himself, "Hello Chris," in response
to meeting his grandmother for the first time, to getting his
first hair-cut, and when asked to finish his dinner. His parents
often felt that Chris was unaware of his surroundings and that
he showed no desire to change.

One particularly unfortunate aspect of autism is the
tendency for self-destructive behavior, such as Chris' scratching.
Such self-stimulating behavior is common in autistic children.
No one knows the true causes of such behavior. However,
many experts hypothesize that it may be inadvertently reinforced through attention. The parent or teacher may comfort,
scold, protect, or embrace the child who is showing self-destructive behavior. Such attention usually provides ample incentive
for the child to continue such activity.

Most teachers notice a drastic difference in the language
capacities of autistic and normal children. Autistic children

display self-centered approaches to language, and their speech is generally oriented to form rather than content. These children are more responsive to speech sounds than to word meanings. They often echo questions and phrases verbatim. This behavior, referred to as echolalia, in some ways resembles their tendency to copy actions (apraxia).

Approximately three fourths of autistic children have IQ scores below 70. These scores lie in the borderline retarded range of intelligence. However, there is some doubt regarding the validity of these tests, since language is a critical factor in assessing intelligence.

The psychologist who evaluated Chris concluded that his chances of making a "normal" childhood adjustment were slim. However, the prognosis of a suitable adult adjustment is slightly more favorable, since many autistic children grow into responsible, productive citizens. The extent to which adequate adjustment is achieved varies greatly. It is discouraging, though, to note that approximately 50 percent of children diagnosed as autistic remain institutionalized throughout their lives. Successful adjustment is more likely for autistic children with higher IQs, better quality speech, and intensive schooling.

The causes of this tragic disorder are obscure and speculative. It has been thought that parents of autistic children are cold, distant, reserved, and intellectual. The name *refrigerator parent* has often been used to describe them. This view has been largely discounted by new scientific studies that have provided other explanations. The fact that a fifth to a quarter of autistic children have a history of brain disease is suggestive of a biological determinant. Other scientists have attributed autism to hereditary and biochemical factors. One particular school of thought contends that autism is due to a difference in brain anatomy in which a certain area of the brain is abnormally large. Finally, it has been suggested that the brains of autistic children function much like a broken computer. That is, signals received by the brain are confused by improper mechanical functioning that distorts both perception and behavior.

The question of teachers' and parents' treatment of Chris' "special" problem arises at this point. They are trying to show him how to care for himself by teaching grooming, safety, toileting, and other self-help skills. A speech pathologist is teaching Chris to communicate through the use of sign language originally created for deaf people. A behavior therapist is increasing the amount of appropriate behavior through shaping techniques, using raisins, cereal, orange juice, colored discs, and other rewards.

Autistic children should be referred to highly qualified professionals who specialize in treating this disorder. The severity of the disorder and the complexity of therapy programs dictate treatment only by those professionals with an unusual degree of expertise in the field. Unfortunately, only limited improvement may be expected with even the very best treatment.

CHILDHOOD SCHIZOPHRENIA

Janis is an eleven-year-old who was referred to the child guidance clinic by her teacher. She is increasingly withdrawn and avoids most people. The quality of her relationships with other children is extremely poor. Her thinking is disorganized. She gives incomplete and unusual answers to questions. Janis is beginning to hear the voice of her father, who died three years ago. Janis does not show excitement or sadness like other children, and her emotions are usually displayed in the form of inappropriate giggling. Her teacher decided to refer her for treatment upon discovering that Janis had drawn a picture of a child wielding a dagger with blood dripping from the blade.

Janis comes from a poor family, and some of the neighbors report that her grandmother is "crazy." Janis' diagnosis of childhood schizophrenia was given by the clinic's consulting psychiatrist.

Literally translated, the term *schizophrenia* means "splitting of the mind." This is not to be confused with the popular notion that schizophrenia is synonymous with "split" or multiple personality. The term *split* as originally used to refer to the separation of thought and emotion that Swiss psychiatrist Eugene Bleuler noticed in some of his disturbed patients around 1911. Schizophrenia is generally considered to be a thought disorder in which thinking is "loose" and disorganized. Probably the most common characteristic observed in schizophrenic persons is withdrawal from social contacts. Many children diagnosed as schizophrenic are shy, timid, and sensitive. Their emotional tone is usually flat or incongruous with the present circumstances. Some schizophrenic children experience hallucinations (primarily auditory and tactile) and paranoid or fantastic delusions that persist beyond normal fantasy activity. Facial grimacing, unusual posturing, and repetitive motor movements are sometimes observed.

Schizophrenia is distinguished from autism in several ways. First, the age of onset is much earlier for autistic children (0 to 2 years), whereas true schizophrenia is rarely seen before the age of ten. Schizophrenic children tend to show blunted emotions, hallucinations, and delusions, whereas autistic children show poor eye contact, complete lack of social interest in people, echolalia, and hyperactivity.

As in the case of autism, efforts to determine specific causes of schizophrenia have been unsuccessful. There is, however, increasing evidence that schizophrenia may have a genetic (inherited) component that causes the disorder to surface when the child is subjected to environmental stress. Past attention has largely focused on inconsistent discipline, poverty conditions, and other environmental explanations.

Most schizophrenics hold a poor prognosis of recovery. In some cases (most studies show a figure of around 10 percent), complete remission of childhood schizophrenia is observed. However, many children must undergo highly specialized, long-term, inpatient (hospital or institutional) care, and they may never achieve a "normal" adult adjustment. In rare instances, schizophrenics demonstrate unusual creativity and accomplishment. For example, William Blake, the eminent poet and artist, displayed classic symptoms of schizophrenia.

The primary treatment for schizophrenia is antipsychotic medication such as phenothiazines, thioxanthines, or butyrophenones. Although these drugs do not cure the disorder, they often control the symptoms. Some limited success has been reported by the use of behavior therapy and, to a lesser extent, by using individual and group counseling methods.

Chapter 3

BRAIN DAMAGE AND HYPERACTIVITY

ACUTE BRAIN SYNDROME

Stephanie, an eight-year-old, showed symptoms of confusion tears and grass stains are always apparent on his clothes. Shawn's she had been there before, she appeared to be quite confused in finding her way to the examining room. She could not specify the day of the week, the date, or what she had for breakfast. She complained of a headache and nausea. The doctor noticed that Stephaine appeared drowsy, although she was quite excited during the initial visit the day before. She was referred to a child neurologist, who confirmed that she was experiencing an acute case of organic brain syndrome.

Fortunately, the *acute brain syndromes* are for the most part, reversible. Although there is some damage to the central nervous system through injury or infection, other parts of the brain can compensate for lost functioning in the affected areas. The acute brain syndromes are primarily marked by a "clouding of consciousness," often demonstrated through confusion and disorientation. Some loss of memory and rapid mood swings are often observed. Drowsiness may alternate with excitability. There is sometimes an increasing tendency to display irritability, restlessness, and shortened attention span. As in the case of Stephanie, vomiting and nausea may result.

Stephanie's precarious condition was the result of a head injury sustained in an automobile accident a year ago. There are many causes of acute brain syndrome; some of the most familiar are hypoglycemia, meningitis, encephalitis, and drug intoxication.

Treatment usually involves a great deal of nursing. Most often, tranquilizing drugs only promote the state of confusion and disorientation. A calm environment and the presence of familiar relatives and friends will aid the child's recovery. Further along in the recovery process, special educational attention may be warranted.

CHRONIC BRAIN SYNDROME

Joel is a five-year-old preschooler who was examined by the neuropsychiatrist at University Hospital. Joel's mother discovered that he had destroyed several pieces of chinaware that she has received as a wedding gift several years ago. He was also seen fiercely attacking his three-year-old brother. His language ability had not improved over the past several months, and he was beginning to have more bedwetting episodes and accidental bowel movements. He no longer seems to understand simple directions and has a difficult time concentrating. Joel appears to be physically uncoordinated and is unable to stand on one foot or walk a straight line. Joel was first seen several months ago by his family doctor, who suspected a brain syndrome. The doctor's worst fears were confirmed upon learning that Joel's case of organic brain syndrome was chronic.

A *chronic brain syndrome* is said to be *irreversible* and *progressive*. Perhaps *regressive* is a more accurate term for the process. In these chronic cases, intellectual and social development stops and then reverses. The overall quality of behavior degenerates to earlier, more primitive levels. Personal grooming and hygiene habits diminish. Aggression and destructiveness are often observed. These children may be unusually lethargic and apathetic. Soiling and bedwetting occur more often. There may be evidence of impaired vision, hearing, and muscular coordination.

As in the case of acute disorders, there are numerous potential causes of chronic brain syndrome. These causes are generally attributed to injuries and diseases (genetic, infectious, metabolic, etc.) that lie beyond the scope of this text. Conditions that may cause chronic brain syndrome include Wilson's disease, congenital syphilis, brain tumors, and Huntington's Chorea. Treatment usually involves medical care and self-help education. As the term *chronic* implies, the prognosis for these children is poor.

NONPSYCHOTIC ORGANIC BRAIN SYNDROME

Nonpsychotic organic brain syndrome is a catchall category that has gained popularity in recent years. This disorder is characterized by mood swings, overactivity, and poor attention span. Often, a decrease in intellectual functioning is observed. This category is reserved for those children in whom it is certain that deviant behavior is linked to brain damage.

Epilepsy, a type of nonpsychotic organic brain syndrome, is continuing but not progressive (degenerative). Although many epileptic children display behavioral problems, others make normal adjustments. A large number of these children are afflicted with seizure disorders involving tremors, convulsions, and loss of consciousness. This seizure activity can be controlled and prevented by the administration of such drugs as phenobarbital and Dilantin.

In the event that a seizure is observed, the child should be placed in an open space, free of furniture and sharp objects. A cloth-covered tongue depressor should be available to prevent obstruction of respiratory passages by the tongue. When a seizure occurs, the child's physician should be consulted immediately.

HYPERACTIVITY

Shawn is an eight-year-old who was referred to the local Mental Health Center by his school counselor. Shawn is continually moving about in an aimless manner. He blurts out in class, interrupting the classroom activities several times a day. Shawn constantly fidgets in his chair when he is not running around the room. He is quite irritable and is often involved in playground fighting. His teacher has noticed his tendency to bump into and break objects. He is always seen sporting a new bruise or cut from these kinds of accidents. Academically, Shawn is doing poorly and cannot concentrate. He is having a particularly tough time with reading. Testing shows that his IQ is slightly above average.

Shawn's mother reports that he was an overactive, fussy infant. He never minds well or pays attention to her requests. Shawn is extremely frustrated when he fails to get his way and usually throws a temper tantrum on these occasions. He has been known to wear out a pair of new shoes in two weeks, and tears and grass stains are always apparent on his clothes. Shawn's mother stated that she sometimes wished that he had never been born, and she finds it hard to control her temper when spanking him. The Mental Health Center's child psychologist diagnosed Shawn as hyperactive. The Center's psychiatrist prescribed medication (Ritalin) in order to control his over-activity and impulsiveness. The entire family was treated by the psychologist in counseling sessions that focused on behavior management techniques. Also, several sessions were required to alleviate the tremendous amount of resentment, hostility, and guilt that had developed among the family members.

Hyperactivity has become a popular term among teachers and parents. Many teachers and parents mislabel "difficult" children as hyperactive. This often serves to place the blame for the child's misbehavior on the hyperactivity rather than on the inability of the adult to manage the misbehavior. Although there are varying degrees of hyperactivity, the truly hyperactive child is consistently overactive, distractible, impulsive, and excitable. A large portion of the child's activity is aimless and haphazard. Children who are not hyperactive may show similar levels of activity, yet the normal child's behavior will seem to be more directed or purposeful. Hyperactive children usually show symptoms very early in life. In many instances, hyperactivity may be confused with other disorders, such as hyperthyroidism or lesions of the brain.

As previously mentioned, hyperactive children are over-active. Excess energy, restlessness, and lack of fatigue are characteristics of the hyperactive child. Hyperactive children seem to touch everything in sight—quickly shifting from one object to the next without paying particular attention to any of them. They usually toggle switches and plugs in a seemingly endless manner. These children are often seen opening and closing the refrigerator door or a chest of drawers. Again, these kinds of behaviors are often aimless and devoid of meaning and purpose. Hyperactive children, as might be expected, often wear out their clothes in brief periods of time. Most parents of these children can expect a great deal of unintentional breakage and general destruction of property.

Hyperactive children are easily distracted and show very poor attention spans, along with an inability to concentrate. Shawn's mother described a typical example of his study habits. He was attempting to do his homework when he heard a screeching tire in the street. He ran to the window to investigate this and noticed an unfamiliar dog in the yard. He hurriedly left to chase the dog, which signalled the end of his interest in his homework as well as in the screeching tires.

Impulsiveness, a characteristic of hyperactivity, is denoted by an absence of inhibition and fear. Examples of this kind of behavior include constant interruptions of conversations, darting across the street before stopping to look both ways, taking money from Dad's billfold before considering the consequences, and so on.

Excitability is also a trait found in hyperactive children. Irritability, low tolerance for frustration, temper tantrums, and mood swings are associated with the excitability component of hyperactivity. Due to the unpredictable nature of the children's moods, hyperactive children are frequently treated inconsistently by parents and teachers. Resentment and frustration are evoked by the chaos that the child creates. These feelings may cause guilt and anxiety, which lead to further negative treatment. Thus, the entire interactional pattern among parents, teachers, and hyperactive children becomes negative, destructive, and self-perpetuating.

Normal social and intellectual development is sometimes thwarted by the symptoms of hyperactivity. The child may miss the optimal periods of learning crucial to academic development. All too often, these children begin to view themselves as "problem kids." Self-esteem diminishes, along with performance in critical areas. Some hyperactive children may pursue negative means of gaining attention, which may bring them into conflict with legal authorities and with society in general. It should be noted that this occurs in a minority of hyperactive children. Although many symptoms tend to abate during adolescence and young adulthood, previously missed opportunities for learning may continue to plague the individual indefinitely.

Hyperactivity is a widespread phenomenon in our culture. It has been estimated that a startling six percent of all ten-year-olds in the United States are hyperactive. These children tend to be predominantly male, with most estimates indicating 5 to 8 males for every hyperactive female.

Unfortunately, as in the case of many other psychological disorders, specific causes of hyperactivity have not been discovered. This disorder has been traditionally attributed to abnormal brain and neurological functioning. (This is one reason for including both of these categories in this chapter.) Some physicians have asserted that hyperactivity is due to problems in brain development, problems that may have been caused by anatomical anomalies (abnormalities), infectious disease, or abnormal chromosones. Brain-injured children often show hyperactive traits. (Caution: Hyperactivity should not be confused with the brain syndromes. Hyperactivity is a distinct disorder and not merely a symptom of another disorder.) However, the vast majority of hyperactive children do not have detectable brain damage. For this reason, many professionals began using the phrase *minimally brain-damaged* to describe hyperactive children. This phrase has been largely abandoned today. This diagnosis is extremely difficult to confirm and provides little useful information about a child.

A more promising search for causation lies in the study of brain biochemistry. Several chemicals are responsible for carrying messages from one nerve cell to another in the brain. One such neurotransmitter is norepinephrine. This chemical affects mood, temperature control, hunger, thirst, arousal, and sexual activity. An increase of norepinephrine levels in the brains of hyperactive children tends to have a calming effect that produces a heightened sense of well-being and facilitates the ability to concentrate. In other words, the areas of the brain responsible for slowing down physical functioning are activated by increased norepinephrine. For this reason, mild stimulant drugs, such as Ritalin, are often prescribed. In the event that Ritalin is prescribed, the adult should watch for possible side effects, including skin rash, loss of appetite, nausea, dizziness, headaches, or insomnia. The child should be referred to a physician if any of these conditions is observed. Often, mild doses of tranquilizing drugs, such as Mellaril, are prescribed in order to produce a general calming effect.

Other causes of hyperactivity which have been suggested include genetic problems, hormonal imbalance, and problems in prenatal development. Although there is some evidence to support each of these explanations, there is no general consensus regarding the etiology of hyperactivity. It is, however, generally accepted that hyperactivity is a congenital (present at birth) disorder that originates in the physiology of the child. The problem can be exacerbated by a chaotic and unstable home life. A great deal of family discord, such as excessive yelling, arguing, fighting, or withdrawal of affection, will certainly aggravate the condition. A calm, stable, accepting environment is most helpful for these children.

Initially, the parent of a hyperactive child should consult a pediatrician or family general practitioner. This person should be able to give a specific diagnosis and refer the child to other professionals who can treat hyperactivity. A psychiatrist may prescribe drugs for the child and assist in working through the emotional and communicational problems that may have developed. A psychologist will be able to provide counseling services to both the parents and children. Usually, the psychologist will train the parents in how to manage the child's behavior effectively. Treatment will also focus on establishing more constructive communication patterns and on increasing the child's self-esteem. Psychologists administer tests that detect strengths and weaknesses in intellectual and social functioning. The psychologist is expected to make specific and practical educational recommendations to the teacher. Many schools employ educational specialists who are trained to interpret these tests and to design individual programs for hyperactive children. Speech and hearing specialists may be consulted when a language delay or a hearing deficit is suspected.

Chapter 9 will focus on principles of managing child behavior. These principles may be applied to hyperactive children as well as to children with other kinds of behavior problems.

Chapter *4*

CHILDHOOD DEPRESSION

Marty, an eleven-year-old, was referred to the child psychologist by her teacher. Marty had become increasingly destructive and aggressive and more prone to withdraw when not engaged in these undesirable activities. She often complained of headaches and stomach cramps, for which the family physician could find no physical cause. Marty had very little appetite and had not been eating well for several months. She frequently criticizes herself for minor inadequacies. For example, her teacher heard her say, "I don't have any friends because my Dad and Mom fight a lot"; "I'm a dummy because I failed the last spelling test"; "I'm not pretty"; and "I wish I had never been born." Marty sees little hope that her condition will ever improve, and she does not believe that she can do anything about it. Further investigation reveals that Marty's parents are planning a divorce and that they haven't been getting along for several years. Marty has an older sister whom she feels is treated more favorably. The two have never been close. The psychologist indicated that

21

Marty is experiencing a primary (not caused by external events) depression that requires intensive individual and family counseling. The family physician prescribed antidepressive medication in order to assist Marty's treatment chemically.

This type of *primary depression* is considered, by most professionals, to be rare in children. The symptoms that usually emerge include a generally sad emotional tone, despair, loss of appetite, occurrence of unfounded physical complaints, preoccupation with death, social withdrawal, and, possibly, aggressiveness and destructiveness. Sometimes, slowed motor responses are observed.

Childhood depression can be usefully categorized as *acute* or *chronic*. Clear causes, such as loss of a loved one or divorce, can be pinpointed in the case of *acute depression*. The child may become withdrawn and preoccupied during this period. The acutely depressed individual will usually recover without professional intervention, and this recovery can be facilitated by placing the child in a new supportive environment. *Chronic depression*, on the other hand, is enduring and requires professional attention. No specific causes can be depicted; however, chronically depressed children often have parents who are cold, distant, and rejecting, and who rely heavily on physical punishment in family discipline. These children are more likely to show a loss of appetite and to have difficulty in sleeping. Some researchers contend that an underlying genetic component may be partially responsible for chronic depression.

Doctors Leon Cytryn and Donald McKnew, members of a National Institute of Mental Health research team, report that the most common form of childhood depression is *masked depression*. That is, the depression is often masked by hyperactivity, poor academic and social adjustment, delinquency, physical complaints, or behavior disorders. Clinical judgment and psychological testing may reveal that the child is depressed, even though there are no primary symptoms of depression. The parents of these children are often alcoholics who may react in abusive, rejecting, and deprecating ways toward their children.

Treatment of the depressed child varies with the age and the nature of depression. Younger children may benefit from parent counseling in which the parents are instructed to recognize their tendencies to be rejecting, aloof, or inconsistent in their treatment of the child. Older children may benefit from individual supportive counseling and family therapy oriented toward identifying destructive patterns of communication and replacing them with more positive, constructive interactional styles. In instances of more severe and chronic depression, one of a number of antidepressive drugs may be administered. These drugs are usually classified as tricyclic drugs or monoamine oxidase (MAO) inhibitors. The parent or teacher should recognize that such drugs as Elavil, Triavil, and lithium carbonate are commonly prescribed and that these drugs serve to alleviate depression by altering the levels of certain chemicals in the brain (neurotransmitters).

Whenever depression is identified or suspected, the possibility of suicide should be considered. Although suicide in young children is extremely rare, it is a leading cause of death in adolescents. Interestingly, those who attempt suicide are predominantly females, whereas the successful suicides are more likely to be males. Overdosing on various kinds of medication is the most common mode of suicide; hanging, wrist cutting, or jumping from windows are somewhat rarer methods. Most threats of or attempts at suicide are for the purpose of attracting attention and sympathy rather than being genuine expressions of an intention to end one's life. However, all references (direct or indirect) to suicide should be taken quite seriously. The child should be closely supervised and all potentially dangerous items (e.g., pills, guns, and knives) should be removed from the child's environment. Immediate referral to the family physician or, preferably, to a qualified mental health professional is vital to the child's well-being.

Chapter 5

BEHAVIOR
DISORDERS

DEFINITION

The term *behavior disorder,* as used here, indicates a behavior problem, regardless of the severity. In some cases, behavior problems are so severe that they are considered to be psychological disorders. Because of the widespread existence of behavior problems the contents of this chapter will apply to an extremely large group of children. A behavior disorder or problem, as defined in this book, refers to any learned undesirable or self-defeating pattern of behavior displayed by a child. Obviously, one's attitude about behavior is a reflection of individual values. Since there is considerable variability in personal values, there are great differences of opinion regarding the desirability of behavior. For example, a child's aggressive behavior on the playground may be applauded by some adults and scorned by others. However, there is a general consensus that such behaviors as lying, cheating, and stealing are undesirable. The disorders discussed in this chapter are examples of typical problems presented to mental health professionals. Behavior, for all practical purposes, is learned, and, therefore, it can be altered through learning. There are several ways (paradigms) in which learning occurs, and these will be briefly discussed. Although it is somewhat unconventional to do so, the traditional diagnoses of childhood neuroses and personality (conduct) disorders will be treated as behavior problems and will be meshed into the learning theory perspective. This approach is considered advantageous for several reasons. First, children's behavior patterns are usually transient and situational. It is unnecessary to label a child as neurotic when the problems may suddenly disappear. The behavior of most children is unstable to the extent that the term *personality disorder* is an accurate description of the problem. Personality disorders are enduring, stable patterns of undesirable behavior. Second, psychologists and psychiatrists are increasingly avoiding the use of these labels. The terms *neurosis* and *personality disorder* do not adequately predict treatment strategies and prognoses for children. Additionally, mental health professionals recognize that an unfavorable stigma is associated with these labels. It is certainly in the best interest of the child to have a specific behavior problem rather than a neurosis. Finally, the medical model is not applicable to problems that are a result of learning. Learned, undesirable behavior is not a disease that can be cured through medical treatment.

WAYS OF LEARNING UNDESIRABLE BEHAVIORS

OPERANT CONDITIONING

Throughout the twentieth century, psychologists have accumulated ample evidence that behavior is largely controlled by its consequences. Some of the better known scientists who have studied the effects of the consequences of behavior include J. B. Watson, B. F. Skinner, and Neal Miller. It is true that behavior that is followed by a reward or reinforcer is much more likely to be repeated. For example, if a hungry child discovers delicious cookies on top of the refrigerator, he or she is much more likely to climb on top of the refrigerator the next time hunger pangs occur. If an infant is fed immediately upon crying, the probability of future crying is drastically increased. This is the principle of *positive reinforcement,* and it plays a major role in the development of a child's behavior patterns. Effective reinforcers vary with the child. Some common reinforcers include candy, raisins, praise, money, television, hugs, and kisses. Behavior problems are learned when children are inadvertently reinforced for undesirable behavior. Children often receive more attention for undesirable than for desirable behavior. Attention, whether positive or negative, usually reinforces the behavior.

Psychologists have learned that undesirable behavior can be decreased by ensuring that the behavior is not followed by a reinforcer. This procedure, called *extinction,* is extremely effective in eliminating bad behavior. The most common usage of extinction involves simply ignoring the child when he or she is displaying an undesirable behavior. This approach, coupled with the positive reinforcement procedure, is very effective in producing the desired behavior change.

Another method by which behavior is modified through its consequences is *punishment.* This method suppresses behavior through the immediate application of an aversive stimulus to a specific response. Punishment may produce several unwanted side effects (see Chapter 9); it should be reserved for situations in which a child physically endangers himself or others, e.g., spanking a child for playing with matches.

Procedures that emphasize learning through the consequences of behavior are called *operant conditioning.* Several types of operant conditioning are often combined and applied to several behaviors simultaneously, which results in an extremely complicated procedure. Such a program would most likely by designed by a behavioral psychologist. The important thing to remember is that most behavior disorders are learned and that they can be unlearned through procedures similar to those mentioned above.

CLASSICAL CONDITIONING

Almost everyone is familiar with the experiment in which Ivan Pavlov trained a dog to salivate to the sound of a bell. The bell was paired with (i. e., presented immediately prior to) the presentation of food. The bell, which was previously a neutral stimulus, became a conditioned stimulus for salivating. This finding had far-reaching effects for the development of psychology and learning theory. Many psychologists who were active during the first third of the twentieth century attributed the bulk of human learning to *classical conditioning*. However, classical conditioning is generally limited to behavior that involves reflexes, although many behavior disorders in children are acquired and treated through processes of classical conditioning.

Watson and Rayner, a research team active in the 1920s, experimentally produced a classically conditioned emotional response (fear) in an infant named Albert.[1] At the age of nine months, Albert was presented with a white rabbit, a white rat, a dog, a monkey, a Santa Claus mask, cotton wool, and a burning newspaper. He showed no evidence of fear and made no attempt to withdraw from these situations. Later, Albert

[1]John B. Watson and Rosalie Rayner, "Conditioned Emotional Reactions," *Journal of Experimental Psychology*, vol. III, 1-12.

was confronted with a loud noise (unconditioned stimulus for fear) created by striking a steel bar with a hammer. He made responses—such as crying, whimpering, violent movement, and falling on his side—that are considered indices of fear. During the experimental phase, Albert was presented with the white rat (conditioned stimulus) immediately prior to presentation of the loud noise. As expected, intense fear responses were observed. Subsequently, this fear was displayed in the presence of the white rat, even though the noise was no longer paired with it. Fear responses also generalized to the Santa Claus mask, the cotton wool, the rabbit, and other furry white objects. Thus, fear and anxiety had been classically conditioned. This experiment seems primitive in comparison to later classical conditioning studies; however, it marks a significant breakthrough in the study of classical conditioning and child behavior. This work also offers a plausible explanation for the development of fear and anxiety, which are serious problems for many children. Further development of classical conditioning techniques has resulted in effective treatment approaches for phobias and enuresis, and such techniques can be essential in testing for sensory defects in young children.

Classical conditioning generally focuses on reflexive responses that involve glands and smooth muscles. These tissues are intricately related to emotional responding. In contrast to operant conditioning, classical conditioning concentrates on the antecedents of behavior more than on the consequences of behavior. Both operant and classical procedures are involved in the development of behavior problems in children. However, the operant model is more extensively involved in the acquisition of most childhood behavior disorders.

Although some may disagree, all human behavior cannot be explained in terms of learning theory. Such factors as genetics, biochemistry, and language seriously complicate simplistic explanations of behavior based on learning theory. Yet the advances made through research in classical and operant conditioning have yielded many invaluable tools for the mental health professional. It should be noted that behavioral techniques are particularly suited for children because young people do not possess learning histories as extensive as those of adults. Therefore, child behavior is usually more susceptible to alteration, which is often readily achieved.

MODELING

Modeling is a form of learning in which a child acts in imitation of a social model. Although modeling is often explained in terms of operant learning, its importance demands special mention. The modeling process has unquestionable influence on the development of a child's behavior patterns.

Such undesirable behavior patterns as lying, stealing, aggression, or swearing are, to some extent, attributable to poor models in the child's environment. Children are often observed imitating athletes, singers, and others whom they perceive as possessing status. The child learns to imitate bad behavior as readily as desirable behaviors. Hence, the importance of ensuring that a child is surrounded by positive models cannot be overemphasized.

There has been considerable research involving the processes of modeling and imitation, and many questions have been left unanswered. However, it is becoming increasingly clear that such factors as age, race, and sex have a strong influence on the modeling process. Controversy regarding persistence of the behavior learned in this manner remains. Yet experts agree that the behavior of significant others in the child's environment has considerable impact in shaping the child's behavior.

This discussion of operant conditioning, classical conditioning, and modeling has, by no means, been comprehensive. It has been intended to provide a basis for understanding how certain behavior disorders develop in the child. A discussion of several behavior problems frequently presented to mental health professionals follows.

EXAMPLES OF BEHAVIOR PROBLEMS

AGGRESSIVE BEHAVIORS

Aggressive behaviors are those intended to cause physical or emotional harm to others. The activities are usually accompanied with extreme emotion, both by the aggressor and by those confronted with the aggressive behavior. Common examples of aggression in children include hitting, biting, scratching, pinching, yelling, throwing temper tantrums, and spitting. The consequences of these behaviors usually involve spanking, lecturing, shaming, reasoning, and so on. These are all forms of attention and will most likely act as reinforcers for the aggressive behavior. Simple aggressive behaviors are best managed by isolating the child in *time out* (Time out is an operant conditioning procedure that involves placing a child in a well-lighted and ventilated room for several minutes). A typical graph for the treatment of aggressive behavior is presented in Figure 5.1.

Beyond simple aggressive behaviors, there exists a syndrome (cluster of symptoms) referred to as an *unsocialized aggressive*

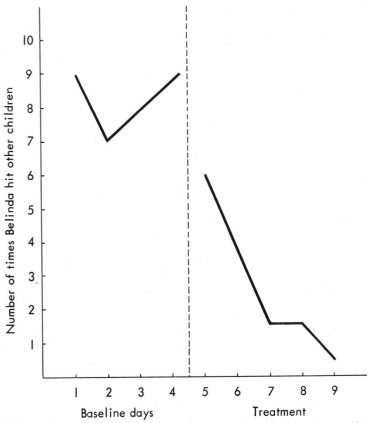

Figure 5.1 Graph of aggressive behavior. The dotted line separates the treatment from the baseline phase.

reaction of childhood. The following is an example of this disorder:

> *Belinda was referred to the mental health center's social worker by the youth court. She is eleven years old and has been arrested twice for stealing cigarettes at a local supermarket. The social worker has learned that Belinda is the third-born child*

*in a family with seven children. Her father is an alcoholic, and
her mother lives on income from welfare and prostitution. The
school reports that Belinda constantly fights with others and
that she frequently lies and cheats on tests. Neighbors contend
that she is sexually promiscuous and that she has been observed
making open sexual advances toward men. She was extremely
resistant and negative during her first visit to the center. Her
utterances were filled with expletives.*

Belinda is experiencing an unsocialized aggressive reaction
of childhood. The American Psychiatric Association's *Diagnostic
and Statistical Manual of Mental Disorders* offers the following
description:

*This disorder is characterized by overt or covert hostile dis-
obedience, quarrelsomeness, physical and verbal aggressiveness,
vengefulness, and destructiveness. Temper tantrums, solitary
stealing, lying, and hostile teasing of other children are common.
These patients usually have no consistent parental acceptance
and discipline. (American Psychiatric Association,* Diagnostic
and Statistical Manual of Mental Disorders, *2nd. [Washington,
D.C.: American Psychiatric Association, 1968], p. 51.)*

The prevalence of this disorder is difficult to determine.
Unsocialized behavior is more common among poor, unintelli-
gent, and divorced persons, among alcohol abusers, and in
children whose parents rely on negative means of discipline.
Although conditioning and modeling play significant roles in
this disorder, many of these children display a neurological
dysfunction. Many of these children are also plagued with
learning disabilities, which tend to exacerbate the problem.

Treatment for this disorder is focused on restructuring
the child's environment in several ways. First, an attempt is
made to teach the child acceptable patterns of assertive be-

havior. This is often achieved through role play and operant techniques. Second, the child is taught to control impulsivity. Such methods as chemotherapy, time-out, and concentration games are employed for this purpose. Third, parents, teachers, and siblings are taught to serve as more appropriate models for the child. Parents are frequently directed to discontinue yelling or hitting the child for misbehavior. Finally, all attempts are made to increase the child's self-esteem. The school is crucial in helping the children learn to view themselves more positively.

DELINQUENT BEHAVIOR

Unlike unsocialized aggressive behavior, *delinquent behavior* is socialized by the child's peer group. Lying, stealing, running away, truancy, and vandalism are examples of delinquent behavior. The child is generally thought to get along well with his or her peers, and extreme aggression and anxiety are not noted. Delinquent behavior is particularly influenced by the modeling and operant processes. These behaviors are encouraged and reinforced by peers and usually elicit considerable attention from parents. It is helpful to demonstrate how delinquent behavior might develop.

Young children are inclined to take things that do not belong to them. They do not understand that it is wrong to pick up an item. Likewise, it is natural for a child to tell tall tales before he or she is capable of discriminating reality and fantasy.

Harold, for example, is an eleven-year-old with an extremely moralistic mother. She hopes that Harold will grow into a morally fine individual. When he was five, Harold picked up a toy fire truck and, clutching it, walked out of the department store. Harold's mother did not notice the fire truck until they reached the car, when she grew quite upset and began to scream at him. Because she was extremely embarrassed, she resisted returning the item to the store. Harold was startled by her reaction and enjoyed the stimulating scene. Several months later, Harold drew a similar response from her by telling a small lie. Harold quickly learned that he could elicit immediate and vehement attention by committing such acts. Two years later, Harold discovered some of the neighborhood children stealing from the department store. He began taking small items, which seemed to please his peers. He has since been apprehended by the police and turned over to the juvenile court, at which time professional help was recommended.

This is a typical example of how mishandling by the parents can result in delinquent behavior. Harold was inadvertently reinforced each time he displayed a natural behavior. It would have been best to explain in a calm, directive tone the reasons why stealing is wrong. Use of the time-out procedure and denial of certain privileges would have been proper when the behavior was repeated. Emotionally laden responses simply reinforce undesirable behavior. Finally, the child knows what upsets adults and will attack this vulnerable area, particularly when angry at the adult.

Delinquent behavior may develop regardless of the parents' good intentions. If lying and stealing progress into delinquent behavior, that behavior may be extremely difficult to extinguish. Additionally, there is considerable reinforcement for delinquent behavior in the child's environment. Children may receive praise from classmates, keep the desirable stolen item, liken themselves to such glorified delinquents as Billy The Kid or John Dillinger, and gain enormous attention from responsible adults. Natural reinforcers for delinquent behavior become tremendously potent when alcohol or drug use is involved. Thus, it is often necessary to remove the child from this reinforcing environment. Attempts should be made to place the child in a setting where appropriate rather than delinquent behavior is encouraged. Lamentably, even residential placement centers cannot entirely eliminate unintentional reinforcers of delinquent behavior.

The role of the mental health professional is to explain to the parents how the child's unacceptable behavior is accidentally reinforced. Principles of operant conditioning and modeling are explained. The mental health professional explores the parents' feelings about the behavior and the reasons for it. Children are usually encouraged to participate in constructive activities that are supervised by responsible adults (appropriate models). Alternative methods of obtaining reinforcement are also explored. Finally, mental health professionals attempt to clarify the acceptable limits of behavior and to prescribe effective contingencies when these limits are exceeded.

FEAR AND ANXIETY

All children experience fear at one time or another. From an evolutionary point of view, *fear* is an adaptive emotional response that prepares an individual for "fight" or "flight." The ability to ward off or flee from an enemy has been critical to the survival of the human race. This behavior is partially based on the fear response. Such events as sudden loud noises, pain, and falling elicit fear in infants. As demonstrated with Albert and the white rat, any number of events can potentially elicit fear through association (pairing) with the stimuli that originally produced the fear response. Hence, a child can learn to fear such things as television, clouds, dogs, music, shadows, snakes, cars, shoes, or any number of items.

The condition is called a *phobia* if the fear escalates to the point of emotionally incapacitating the child. Phobias have traditionally been referred to as neuroses; however, they are considered as behavior problems for the following reasons: First, the fear is learned; second, it is harmful to the child to be labeled neurotic.

It is difficult to estimate the number of children who experience phobias. Phobic children are more likely to come from smaller families with higher educational and socioeconomic levels. Parents of these children tend to be slightly overprotective, in that they support the unrealistic fear. They may show excessive attention and sympathy, or they may assist the child in avoiding those situations that elicit the fear.

Regardless of the way in which the fear develops and is sustained, classical conditioning procedures provide several methods of treatment. One method, extinction, involves placing the child in the situation that evokes the fear. Usually the fear will vanish as a result of repeated exposure to the fear-producing stimulus. *Counterconditioning* is a technique in which the child is encouraged to participate in activities incompatible with fear. Eating is an example. If the fear-evoking stimulus is gradually introduced into the child's environment, the fear will probably extinguish. For example, the white rat could be presented on the opposite side of the room from Albert while he is eating an ice cream cone. Albert would not be physically capable of eating while intensely afraid, and the stronger eating response would eventually dominate the fear response. Children are also trained in systematic relaxation, a procedure that involves an awareness of the body tension associated with fear. They are then taught to relax major muscle groups and to practice these exercises several times a day. Finally, the child is instructed to use the relaxation techniques when confronted with the fearful situation. Obviously, the child cannot be relaxed and afraid simultaneously. Another procedure involves teaching parents not to, in any way, attend to or reinforce the fear. *Anxiety* is considered to be a fear response to many situations. The anxious child shows such a generalized fear that it is impossible to pinpoint the specific stimuli that produce the fear. Anxiety is created by extreme pressure to perform, by punitive discipline, or by inconsistent approaches to child management. The child becomes tense and nervous in a variety of situations because he or she may have previously had noxious experiences when confronted with similar situations. The anxious child may demonstrate numerous physical complaints: weight gain, hyperactivity, or withdrawal, to name a few. Since the emotional components of fear and anxiety are alike, similar treatment techniques are generally applied.

An encouraging aspect of these conditions is that the prognosis is excellent. Studies have concluded that adults treated for phobias or anxiety are no more likely to demonstrate a "mental disorder" than members of the general population. Furthermore, treatments for phobias and anxiety are now quite effective. The advances in treatment are attributed to an increasing sophistication of the scientific study of emotion and behavior.

ENURESIS

Enuresis is considered a behavioral problem because it can be effectively treated through operant and classical conditioning procedures. Enuresis generally refers to the act of involuntarily urinating an average of once or more each month past the age of four. This includes day or night wetting; however, nighttime wetting is far more common. Boys are more likely to have this problem than girls. Approximately 10 to 14 percent of boys between four and ten are enuretic, while only 6 to 9 percent of girls show uncontrolled wetting.

Although enuresis occurs throughout society, it is more common among lower socioeconomic groups. Older enuretic children tend to be physically underdeveloped, to be less intelligent, to have larger families, and to experience more familial turmoil. Interestingly, enuresis is usually not associated with other psychological disorders in children under ten. However, other problems are usually observed in older enuretic children and in children who experience daytime wetting.

The causes of enuresis are extremely complex. The disorder is associated with abnormal physiological dysfunction in a very small percentage of cases. It has been estimated that one-third of enuretic children have experienced a significant stress that triggered the problem. Other studies reveal that enuresis may be an inherited brain mechanism.

Treatment for enuresis has been largely successful. Studies show that nearly 90 percent of enuretic children are cured within six months through the use of currently accepted treatment procedures.

The first step of treatment should involve consultation with a physician. Behavioral strategies will probably be unsuccessful in cases with a physical cause. Such strategies, however, are effective when the cause can be attributed to learning. Once a behavioral approach has been recommended, the therapist should make every effort to actively involve the child in treatment. The child should be asked to describe his or her feelings about the problem. Children should take the responsibility for removing wet materials and placing them in the dirty clothes hamper. Usually, a buzzer connected to a moisture-sensitive pad is used in treatment. The buzzer (unconditioned stimulus) awakens the child immediately after he or she passes the first few drops of urine. The child is required to urinate in the bathroom, change the bedclothes (depending on his or her age), and reset the alarm. Eventually the child begins to awaken in response to bladder tension (conditioned stimulus) instead of in response to the buzzer. This is a classical conditioning procedure. Dry nights should be rewarded with gold stars or other tokens that can be exchanged for mutually chosen rewards. This is an extremely effective program that does not require shaming or other punitive or moralistic approaches.

Antidepressant drugs are sometimes prescribed for children with enuresis. Although these drugs may decrease the frequency of bedwetting, they do not eliminate the condition. Unless a medical condition exists, drugs should be used only after behavioral strategies have failed.

ENCOPRESIS

Encopresis is defined as a condition of persistently soiling (by passing stools) one's clothing after three years of age. Since treatment depends primarily on learning, this disorder is considered a behavior problem. Encopresis is less prevalent than enuresis, yet it is not rare. Like enuresis, this condition is more common in boys.

Very little research has been accumulated on the causes of encopresis. Treatment for this condition should begin with a thorough medical examination. In the event that a physical disorder is not indicated, treatment should proceed in much the same manner as for enuresis. The child's feelings about the condition and his or her motivation for improvement should be explored. He or she should be responsible for cleaning soiled clothing. The child should be required to sit on the toilet for two daily ten-minute sessions; a kitchen timer may be used to signal the end of the interval. These sessions should occur at approximately the same time each day: A few minutes after eating is often optimal, due to increased bowel activity. Successful bowel movements are rewarded with tokens that can be traded for some desired object or event. Since encopretic children often have problems with constipation, administration of mineral oil or some other mild laxative is helpful. In some cases, the use of enemas is indicated. Although soiling can cause embarrassment and other unpleasant social consequences, punitive approaches to treatment are ineffective and are potentially harmful to the child.

EATING PROBLEMS

Overeating and associated problems have reached epidemic proportions in the United States and many other countries. More than ever before, voluminous amounts of high calorie foods are easily accessible to the vast majority of citizens of industrialized nations. The problem of overeating is by no means exclusive to adults.

Eating is a behavior that is clearly influenced by the processes of modeling and operant conditioning. Children are likely to imitate the eating patterns of parents and other influential figures. If a boy's father piles loads of high calorie foods on his plate and gulps them down at a rapid pace, the child is likely to do the same. In-between-meal eating is also influenced by the parents' example. To further complicate the situation, eating is usually a reinforcing activity in and of itself. Administering certain foods as reinforcers for certain behaviors is a common procedure. However, the most immediately reinforced response is eating rather than the behavior in question.

Barring a physical condition, poor eating habits usually result from the parents' mishandling of the child's eating behavior. For example, requiring a child to "clean" his or her plate prior to serving dessert teaches the child to overeat. Most parents do not realize that children will select the types and amounts of food that their bodies require at a given time. Fighting or struggling over the child's eating habits is unnecessary and may create poor eating habits later in life.

Proper eating patterns are conveyed in several ways. First, it is essential to set a proper example for the child. Second, high calorie junk foods should not be purchased and/or made accessible to the child. A reasonable array of appropriate foods should be presented to the child. Complete freedom of selection of the type and amount of food taken should be exercised. Provided that high calorie foods are inaccessible and that parents demonstrate appropriate eating patterns, an eating problem is not likely to result.

If the child is overweight or obese, he or she should be initially referred to the family doctor. The child's metabolic and general physical functioning will be evaluated. Once a physical problem has been ruled out, referral to a behavioral psychologist should be considered. Usually, the parents will be asked to list the kinds and amounts (in calories and grams) of food ingested on a daily basis. The parents will also be asked to report times, places, and conditions of eating. Initially, no attempt is made to change the child's eating patterns. This is called the baseline or observation period.

After the baseline period has ended, the treatment phase begins. The child will normally be asked to reduce caloric intake by approximately three hundred to five hundred calories daily. This is often done by helping the child to avoid eating in certain situations, such as after school or while watching television. The child is praised lavishly whenever a family member or friend notices that the child is eating appropriate foods at the specified rate and time. Concrete rewards, such as a toy or money, should be given for appropriate eating. The point is to provide other reinforcers that compete with the reinforcing value of food. The child should lose weight gradually (one to two pounds per week) until the optimal weight, determined by the child's age and height, is achieved. Professionals who administer weight reduction programs will have standardized charts that specify optimal weight levels. Finally, the child should maintain balanced diets through choosing from meats, cereals (breads), dairy products, vegetables, and fruits.

Another problem that may develop is refusal to eat for an extended period of time. This condition is commonly called *anorexia nervosa* and is displayed most often by adolescent females; it is rare in children. However, if a child refuses to eat for more than two or three days, a physician or psychologist should be consulted immediately. This is a psychological disorder that can lead to death if untreated. These children may literally starve themselves to death. The causes of this condition are unknown.

In summary, parents and teachers should be aware of how behavior problems are learned and eliminated. Although some behavior problems may be more serious than others, proper diagnosis and referral is critical to effective treatment. Finally, it has been demonstrated that labeling can be harmful to a child's development and that it should be avoided in favor of observing and recording specific behavior patterns.

Chapter **6**

MENTAL RETARDATION

DEFINITION

Mental retardation is a very general category of disorders that includes persons with below average intellectual and adaptive abilities. The American Association of Mental Deficiency (AAMD) has offered the following definition:

> *Mental retardation refers to significant subaverage general intellectual functioning existing concurrently with deficits in adaptive behavior, and manifested during the developmental period. (In N. Robinson and H. Robinson,* The Mentally Retarded Child *[New York: McGraw-Hill, 1976]).*

Let us examine this definition more closely. First, emphasis is on present behavior. An individual's level of functioning in the past or expected level of functioning in the future is irrelevant

45

to current classification. Second, the level of intellectual functioning is usually ascertained by a standardized intelligence
test. The two most widely accepted and employed tests for
children are the *Wechsler Intelligence Scale for Children (Re-
vised)* and the *Stanford-Binet Intelligence Scale.* Third, this
definition does not differentiate mental retardation from other
childhood psychological disorders. For example, a child may
be classified as both autistic and mentally retarded. Finally,
the child's success in coping with developmental tasks should
be considered in diagnosing mental retardation.

Since the degree of mental retardation varies widely,
subcategories have been developed. In the nineteenth century
and the early twentieth century, the terms *moron, imbecile,*
and *idiot* were used to distinguish various degrees of mental
retardation. More humane terms, including *mild, moderate,
severe,* and *profound,* are currently used by professionals in
this area. Depending on the specific test used, IQ scores may
partially determine how a child is classified; this, in turn,
influences his or her placement in the educational system.
Generally, children with IQs in the mid-fifty to upper sixty
range are considered mildly retarded, those with lower forty to
mid-fifty range scores are termed moderately retarded, those
with mid-twenty to lower forty range scores are labeled severely
retarded, and children with below twenty to twenty-five range
scores are classified as profoundly retarded. It is important
to reiterate that these scores must be substantiated by measures
of adaptive behavior in order to *legally* and *ethically* determine
the presence and/or the degree of mental retardation. Adaptive
measures often employed are the *Vineland Social Maturity
Scale* and the *AAMD Adaptive Behavior Scale.* Unfortunately,
many parents do not stress the development of skills required
for adequate performance on intelligence tests. However, all
children are expected to develop such abilities as toileting,

motor coordination, knowledge of dangerous situations, and the like in order to adapt to their respective environments. These types of skills are measured by adaptive behavior scales.

PREVALENCE

Approximately 3 percent of all children in the United States are mentally retarded. Although levels of intelligence generally follow the "normal (frequency) curve," there are a disproportionate number of individuals found in the low end of the continuum (moderately to profoundly retarded). This phenomenon is a reflection of serious impairment caused either by brain injury or by genetic disorders. There are more retarded males than females. Males are more vulnerable to many genetic disorders because of specific differences in chromosomal structure unique to males. Finally, mental retardation is usually detected in the early school years because these children are unable to cope with normal academic and social demands.

CAUSES

The causes of mental retardation are legion and include genetic (inherited) disorders as well as a variety of environmental conditions.

A person's physical characteristics are inherited through the genes of his or her parents. These genes are found on the chromosomes in each cell of the body and in the reproductive cells. The body cells contain forty-six chromosomes arranged in twenty-three pairs. Sex cells (the male sperm cell and the female egg cell) have twenty-three chromosomes, representing one member of each pair of the twenty-three pairs in the body cells. Thus, the full forty-six chromosomes are found in the fertilized egg due to a combination of male and female sex cells. From that point, the fertilized egg goes through a process of cell division called *mitosis,* in which a genetic replica is produced. This process of cell division occurs repeatedly, under the guidance of certain chemicals deoxyribonucleic acid (DNA) and ribonucleic acid (RNA). Upon sexual maturity, the individual will be capable of a special kind of cell division known as *meiosis.* This process involves the original cell (46 chromosomes) splitting in half (23 chromosomes) to form the male sperm cell or the female egg cell.

Genetic codes are responsible for such characteristics as gender; hair, eye, and skin color; fingerprint patterns; and color blindness. Genetic make-up partially determines height, weight, physical appearance, intelligence level, athletic ability, and a host of other variables. The environment, however, has some influence on the outcome of these factors.

Obviously, genetic transmission is extremely complex, and errors may occur throughout the process. For example, mistakes often occur during cell division, causing the transmission of too much or too little chromosomal material. Occasionally, new forms of specific genes (*mutations*) are created, which may work to the benefit as well as to the detriment of the species. There may be specific genes that are responsible for certain types of *genetic syndromes.* Each type of error may cause mental retardation.

The most common type of moderate to severe mental retardation is *Down's Syndrome,* popularly known as *mongolism.* This disorder is also referred to as *Trisomony 21,* because there is an additional chromosome attached to the number 21 chromosomal pair. This condition is caused by incomplete separation of chromosomes during the process of meiosis (division of reproductive cells). One in every 660 births results in Down's

Syndrome; however, risks are significantly higher in the event of a family history of this disorder and if the mother is thirty-five or older. Common symptoms include slanted eyes; small ears, nose, and mouth; square hands; short fingers; obesity; and underdeveloped genitalia. These individuals invariably experience some degree of mental retardation. Curiously, afflicted individuals generally display an affectionate, friendly, and relaxed personality style.

There are a wide variety of genetic disorders that cause mental retardation. Some of these, such as *inherited metabolic disorders,* are treatable, to the extent that mental retardation can be prevented if the disorder is detected soon after birth. Many types of genetic disorders may be detected during pregnancy through a procedure called *amniocentesis.* This procedure involves inserting a needle in the abdominal area of the pregnant woman in order to obtain a sample of amniotic fluid. Examination of the fluid's chromosomal material yields data about the genetic make-up of the unborn child. Pregnancy is often terminated when a genetic disorder is discovered.

In addition to genetic disorders, mental retardation may be caused by certain conditions in the child's prenatal (before birth) and postnatal (after birth) environments. *Prenatal conditions* that may cause mental retardation include poor maternal nutrition, maternal infection, maternal age (too young or too old), exposure of the mother to excessive amounts of radiation, or excessive use of alcohol and other drugs. *Postnatal factors* that may produce mental retardation include head injuries; infections, such as meningitis and encephalitis; or ingestion of poison.

Perhaps the most common cause of the milder forms of mental retardation is the general lack of meaningful stimulation in the child's environment. Children whose parents lack adequate language skills and fail to satisfy the child's emotional needs are likely to demonstrate this kind of mental retardation. Once critical learning periods have passed, it is extremely difficult, if not impossible, for the child to function normally later in life. This type of mental retardation is often referred to as *cultural-familial retardation* and is most prevalent among poor families and among children in rural areas.

TREATMENT

The treatment of mental retardation is a long and tedious process. Mental retardation cannot be cured, and gains with these children are often painfully gradual. Frequently, severely to profoundly retarded people require residential placement. This type of treatment may depend on the ability and willingness of the family to care for the child.

Treatment for the retarded child within his or her community usually involves an intensive educational effort. For many retarded children, behavior modification techniques have been found to be useful in training basic language, social, and self-help skills. Presently, there is an educational trend, called *mainstreaming,* to place retarded children with higher functioning in normal classroom settings rather than in special education classes. There is no evidence that isolating retarded children facilitates their learning process, nor that the presence of retarded children in the classroom setting interferes with the learning rates of the "normal" students. Mainstreaming attempts to provide the least restrictive environment possible for retarded children. Association with these children is also considered to provide positive learning experiences for the "normal" students.

Unfortunately, mentally retarded children display a greater number of different types of psychological disorders than their nonretarded counterparts. Parents and teachers often unwittingly believe that certain deviant behavior is part of the overall disorder. This oversight may result in the unnecessary persistence of undesirable behaviors which, in turn, may lead to residential placement that could have been avoided. Parents should consult qualified educational and mental health professionals in order to outline realistic expectations and treatment strategies. Professional counseling is often required to assist the parent in coping with the special problems and demands that arise in parenting the retarded child. It is helpful to explore the patterns of denial, guilt, frustration, resentment, and depression that are commonly expressed by the parents of retarded children.

Chapter 7

LEARNING
DISABILITIES

Jeff is an eight-year-old third grader who has recently been placed in a self-contained learning disabilities classroom. Although he was found to have "normal intelligence," his progress in school has been painfully slow. Jeff's reading vocabulary is restricted to approximately five words; thus, his performance is impaired in all subjects that require a minimal reading aptitude. The school psychologist suggested that his poor school performance has created social and emotional problems, which have been observed by his parents and teachers. For example, Jeff rarely plays cooperatively with his schoolmates and has recently become disruptive in the classroom. He is easily frustrated, and his attention span fades rapidly when he is confronted with even the most simple tasks. The teacher of learning disabled children recommended initially that Jeff attend school for only half a day. He will gradually increase the length of time he spends in school each day as he demonstrates a more favorable adjustment to the classroom. He is

*currently involved in such activities as arranging letter-blocks
so that they spell simple words. The teacher is careful to stimulate all of his sensory channels in teaching basic reading skills.
Also, there is an emphasis on teaching basic social skills so that
Jeff will be able to interact more appropriately with his peers.
The educational process promises to be fraught with frustration
and discouragement; however, everyone hopes that Jeff will
emerge relatively unscathed.*

DEFINITION

Jeff is experiencing a *learning disability* (LD), which is a complex
and difficult to understand disorder. The specific characteristics of a learning disability vary with the child and are rarely,
if ever, identical in any two children. The concept of learning
disabilities has evaded precise definition. Widespread disagree-
ment exists among learning disability experts concerning the
nature and cause of these disorders. Estimates of the prevalence
of learning disabled children range from one to fifteen percent
of the population below eighteen years of age.

The National Advisory Committee on Handicapped
Children has offered one of the clearest and most comprehensive definitions of learning disabilities:

> *Children with special learning disabilities exhibit a disorder in
> one or more of the basic psychological processes involved in
> understanding or in using spoken or written languages. These
> may be manifested in disorders of listening, thinking, talking,
> reading, writing, spelling, or arithmetic. They include condi-
> tions which have been referred to as perceptual handicaps,
> brain injury, minimal brain dysfunction, dyslexia, developmental
> aphasia, etc. They do not include learning problems which are
> due primarily to visual, hearing, or motor handicaps, to mental
> retardation, emotional disturbance, or to environmental dis-
> advantage.*

Note that, according to the definition, a learning disability is essentially an inability to understand or use language effectively. Further, this inability is a deficit in and of itself and is not the result of another handicapping condition.

CAUSES

There are numerous causes of learning disabilities. Even in individual cases, causative factors are difficult to determine, but one cause involves inappropriate teaching methods, particularly in the elementary grades. Teachers may simply fail to emphasize the prerequisite skills for effective mastery of language. Evaluation of the curricular content experienced by learning disabled children often reveals poor instructional programming, lack of motivating activities, or a narrow range of activities during the early school years. The fact that inadequate teaching methods may cause learning disabilities presents a special challenge to those responsible for the education of our children.

Learning disabilities are often caused by environmental influences, such as poor nutrition, accidents, illness, lack of coherent sensory stimulation, or inadequate exposure to language during the preschool years. Also, sound emotional development is essential to efficient learning. Learning disabilities are also frequently caused by deficiencies in basic cognitive processes, such as perception, recall, and concept formation. These processes are critical to the understanding, association, and expression of information. The *Illinois Test of Psycholinguistic Abilities* and the *Purdue Perceptual Motor Survey* are tests commonly used to identify specific deficiences in the cognitive processes.

Many experts contend that genetic factors are involved in learning disabilities. It was found, in one study of 116 children labeled *dyslexic* (having reading, spelling, and writing difficulties), that 88 percent of these children had other family members with learning disabilities. However, there remain substantial differences in opinion about the nature and extent of genetic involvement in learning disabilities.

Several metabolic disorders have been implicated in the development of learning disabilities. Two of the more familiar biochemical disorders associated with learning disabilities are *hypoglycemia* and *hypothyroidism*. The evidence that biochemical conditions may cause learning disabilities is highly speculative. However, the use of dietary control and medication has provided limited improvement for certain types of learning disabilities. These techniques have been applied to hyperactivity, attentive behavior, and distractability, but they remain in the experimental stages.

TYPES OF LEARNING DISABILITIES

Perceptual disorders are diagnosed as the cause of learning disability in many children. *Perception* is the ability to recognize and integrate stimuli so that meaning is extracted from the environment. Information is obtained through vision, hearing, touch, taste, smell, and body position. Although all of the senses are involved in learning, *visual* and *auditory perception* are the most important processes involved in understanding language. Problems of visual perception include *inabilities in perceiving form, figure-ground discriminations,* or *spatial relationships*. Furthermore, *visual-motor integration* and *visual discrimination* are critical aspects of visual perception. A difficulty in one or more of these areas may interfere with the child's ability to see or write words correctly. Likewise, problems in *auditory figure-ground association, auditory discrimination, auditory memory*, and *auditory blending* (synthesizing sounds into a word) impair the child's ability to understand and produce language. There are several tests that accurately pinpoint problems in visual and auditory perception. These tests guide the learning disabilities specialist in selecting one or more of the available remedial programs. Examples of these programs include *The Frostig Program for the Development of Visual Perception* or *Sound Order Sense,* which is a program designed for children with difficulties in auditory perception. Skillful, systematic application of these strategies often greatly improves serious perceptual handicaps.

It has become apparent that movement is an integral part of the learning process. Psychologists indicate that learning is an *active* rather than a passive phenomenon. Movement has generally been placed into two classes: *gross motor skills* and *fine motor skills. Gross motor coordination* includes such activities as walking, running, jumping, and balancing on one leg. These skills increase the range of activities potentially available to the child and enhance the child's ability to explore his or her environment. *Fine motor skills* include intricate eye and hand movements and coordination of the movements. Fine motor skills are required for reading, writing, or drawing. An inability to produce smooth, coordinated, horizontal eye movements would obviously cause a reading disability. Tests have been designed to accurately assess gross and fine motor abilities. Subsequent to discovering a motor deficiency, the learning disabilities teacher implements a systematic remedial program to improve the child's motor coordination.

As previously mentioned, there are a variety of conditions that may potentially impair a child's ability to use symbols effectively. For example, it is believed that children must establish a concrete image that represents a word or symbol before the word can be meaningfully used. This is part of a process called *inner speech*. For a child to comprehend the word "apple," he or she must have an internal image of an apple. An inability to form the image will produce incorrect uses of the word. Further, the child must be able to produce an image of an apple in response to the spoken word. This process is called *auditory receptive language* and can be extremely difficult for some children. A deficiency in language reception is referred to as *sensory aphasia, receptive aphasia,* or, simply, *word deafness.* For language to be complete, the child must accurately receive and express words. Difficulties in *auditory expressive language* may be labeled *expressive aphasia* or *motor aphasia.* Receptive or expressive aphasia is sometimes found to be directly linked to brain dysfunction localized in the language area of the cortex (Wernicke and Broca's area).

There are many other processes in which language can be affected. Examples include perceiving speech sounds, formulating words and sentences, word selection, word sequencing, and the like. These processes may limit the child's competency in spelling, arithmetic, written language, and other academic areas.

TREATMENT

Treatment of the learning disabled child requires the expertise of a wide variety of professional disciplines. Pediatricians, opthamologists, psychologists, neurologists, educators, speech pathologists, and psychiatrists have been traditionally responsible for treatment of these children. A complex disorder such as a learning disability demands a multidisciplinary approach in the identification, diagnosis, and treatment of these children. The teacher is the single most important professional involved in the treatment of a learning disabled child. He or she is responsible for implementing the recommendations of the other experts as well as for effectively administering highly individualized educational strategies. Several programmed treatment strategies are listed in Appendix VI.

Although a detailed discussion of the various treatment strategies is beyond the scope of this chapter, two popular approaches will be briefly mentioned. R. H. Barsch developed a theory and resulting treatment strategy termed *movigenics*. This theory states that movement is the basis for learning and that a deficiency in motor skills results in a cognitive disturbance. Hence, treatment of the learning disabled child focuses solely on motor development and "motor efficiency." Although the movigenic curriculum has enjoyed some popularity, the evidence in support of this approach is sparse and is insufficient to warrant the use of movigenics as a sole strategy in the treatment of learning disabilities.

Another strategy for treating the learning disabled child is the *Doman-Delacato approach*. This method stresses the concept of "neurological organization," which is necessary for optimal development. According to this approach, a learning disability results from a neurological disorganization, apparently caused by a variety of factors. Treatment includes an activity, called *patterning*, that involves precise movements of the arms, legs, and head. The objective of these movements is to stimulate brain cells, which, in some way, produces neurological organization. Although widely applied, the Doman-Delacato method has been the subject of severe criticism. This approach has not been substantiated by acceptable scientific research.

Presently, the most effective remedial techniques for learning disabilities attack the specific learning problem only after a meticulous diagnostic evaluation. The recommended educational strategies are highly individualized and evidence considerable variability from one child to the other. Any one curriculum purported to be the preferred treatment for learning-related disorders should be held suspect by teachers, parents, and other responsible adults.

Chapter **8**

GETTING
HELP

WHEN TO SEEK PROFESSIONAL HELP

There is considerable variability in children's behavior, and it is often difficult to decide whether professional help with a problem is justified. This decision is easy only when a child is showing a serious problem. Frequently, the parent or teacher hesitates to refer a child when the problem appears less serious. Facts to consider include the financial commitments, the time demands, the risk of stigma sometimes associated with treatment, and the prognosis for the effectiveness of treatment. These concerns frequently prevent an afflicted child from entering therapy. On the other hand, many parents and teachers inadvertently refer children who are experiencing normal "growing pains." Although this type of error is far less serious than failure to refer when warranted, knowledge of behaviors that require professional attention is essential to making appropriate referrals. Finally, many parents use their children as an entree into a professional's office to deal with problems that actually concern the adult. In order to avoid exploiting the child who does not require treatment, parents should investigate their motivations for seeking treatment.

It is important to note that all children experience significant problems en route to becoming adults. Most of these adjustment problems are transient and insignificant. Young children will usually demonstrate one or more of such traits as withdrawal, excessive worry, disobedience, excessive aggressiveness, shame, and nightmares. Specific behavior problems may include temper tantrums, bedwetting, soiling, and thumbsucking. Such behavior does not automatically mean that the child has a psychological disorder. Children are quite resilient and adaptable, and these types of problems often improve without professional intervention. Excessive parental concern may cause the behavior to persist. On the other hand, the behavior problem that continues should not be lightly dismissed. Parents must be alert to the balance between worry and complacency.

One of the keys to recognizing a disturbance is the persistence of the behavior. For example, if a first-grade child is having difficulty discriminating among the letters of the alphabet during the first few weeks of school, a referral would be unwarranted. However, if no progress is observed after three or four months, referral may be proper. Stealing is a good example. Most children will, at some point, take an item that does not belong to them. A professional referral is unnecessary in response to the first or second occurrence of stealing. However, if a pattern of stealing emerges, professional help is certainly indicated.

There are several general questions that should be asked prior to making a decision to refer a child for mental health-related treatment.

1. Is the child behaving in a similar manner to children his or her age? As stated, there are considerable individual differences in children's abilities and in the appropriateness of their behavior. However, if extreme differences between the child in question and other children the same age are observed, a disorder may be present. If a three-year-old child cannot produce short sentences when its siblings were talkative at the same age, a professional referral would be in order. Although occasional squabbles are common among most children, constant fighting should arouse suspicion. There are general limits of acceptable behavior that are partially determined by the behavior of the child's peers. Sound judgment and common sense usually result in decisions that are best for the child.

2. The child's ability for self-control is another factor that should be considered in making a referral. The term *self-control* is used in the broadest sense and generally refers to the child's ability to direct his or her behavior. Children who act on impulse and whose behavior never seems to result from internal cues may be experiencing one of several types of disorders. Internal cues may include visual images, self-verbalization, relaxation responses, and other types of self-produced stimuli. Distractability, running away, extreme aggressive behavior, daytime wetting or soiling past toilet training, and excessive selfishness may be considered characteristic of impulsive behavior. It is important to arrange the consequences of this behavior in such a manner as to reduce the frequency of occurrence. This task frequently requires the expertise of a mental health professional.

3. How well does the child adjust to the home and school environment? Adequate functioning within the home and school is imperative to the child's general well-being. These are the places where the child absorbs most of the experience required for independent adult living. Children are expected to get along reasonably well with peers and siblings. Excessive

withdrawal, dependence, or aggression may indicate social ineptitude. Some degree of social responsiveness is required for the child to learn many important lessons taught through play. Children are also expected to grow and learn through experiences encountered at home and in school. The child's behavior may show that he or she is not benefiting from experience. In such cases, a learning disability or phobia, mental retardation, or a behavior disorder may be present. Poor adjustment within the home or school may be indicative of any number of problems that could demand professional attention.

4. What is the *quality* of the child's emotional responses? Excessive crying, enduring nightmares, significant loss of appetite, sleeplessness, persistent irritability, temper tantrums, and phobias should evoke concern among parents and teachers. Again, it is helpful to judge the level of a child's emotional maturity in relation to others approximately the same age. The kinds of problems mentioned above may inhibit normal development and create an atmosphere of apprehension and dissatisfaction. Unnecessary stress is placed on all of the family members as well as on others who are responsible for the child's well-being.

There are many physical indicators of emotional stress. Adults must be aware of recurring physical complaints, the causes of which cannot be discovered by the family physician. Headaches, dizziness, frequent stomach pains, nausea, and constipation are several physical symptoms that are often caused by stress. These are usually caused by significant changes in the child's environment. Common examples include divorce or separation, a death in the family, bringing a newborn sibling home from the hospital, moving to another location, or merely transferring to a different school. Sometimes the stresses that evoke physical symptoms are more subtle and become apparent only after careful study. Each child responds uniquely to his or her environment, particularly in situations which produce stress.

5. Are there any peculiarities in the child's physical development? Extreme variation in the size and shape of the body parts should be noted. Specific areas of interest include head circumference and the size and shape of eyes, hands, and feet. Irregularities in these areas may suggest some type of genetic disorder. The child's motor coordination should be compared to others approximately the same age. Lack of coordination is often characteristic of mental retardation or a learning disability. The family physician should be consulted concerning the child's weight in relation to both age and height. It is important to look for radical shifts in weight and eating patterns. These data are extremely helpful to mental health professionals and may help to confirm a diagnosis of a psychological disorder.

6. Has the child ever displayed a seizure or convulsions? Seizure activity is an extremely serious neurological dysfunction. However, seizures can generally be controlled with medication. A seizure may take the form of violent spastic movements coupled with loss of consciousness and total lack of motor control. On the other hand, a brief staring spell during which the child is unresponsive to external stimulation may represent seizure activity. When these behaviors are observed, the child should be immediately taken to a physician. The doctor may do an electroencephalogram (EEG) and/or a brain scan. These are painless procedures and pose no risk to the child.

Other signs of possible neurological disorders include intense recurring headaches, lethargy, daytime wetting or soiling, periods of unresponsiveness, tremor activity, and memory lapses. Although these problems are usually physiological, learning and emotional problems may exist concomitantly.

In summary, there is overlap in the general areas of behavior that may indicate a psychological disorder. These categories are by no means exhaustive. They are intended to help the responsible adult organize his or her approach to making a reliable assessment of the child. The adult should focus on (1) significant differences in the child's behavior relative to age, (2) degree of self-control, (3) learning and social behavior exhibited at home and in school, (4) emotional tone, (5) physical development, and (6) neurological indicators. The parent, teacher, minister, or guidance counselor is reminded to look for enduring patterns of behavior rather than for transient situational reactions. Given the above information, coupled with reasoning, sound judgment, and common sense, the adult will be able to make referrals confidently and sensibly.

WHO CAN HELP

Many of the problems associated with children's psychological disorders can be effectively treated by the family doctor, the teacher, or the knowledgeable parent. Frequently, however, the child's behavior may require more specialized treatment by mental health professionals. Lamentably, the mental health field has been fertile ground for charlatans, particularly because of recent expansion and the lack of clear definition and organization. But standardization of the qualifications of mental health professionals is becoming more prevalent, and the quality of services provided to the consumer is generally improving. An excellent guide to mental health services has been offered by Clara Claiborne Park and Dr. Leon N. Shapiro. Their book, entitled *You Are Not Alone,* offers clear, comprehensive, and reliable information concerning the nature of mental problems and how to get help for them.

As Park and Shapiro point out, the primary mental health professionals include psychiatrists, psychoanalysts, psychologists, social workers, nurses, and paraprofessionals.

A *psychiatrist* is a medical doctor (M.D.) who specializes

in emotional problems and mental illness (medical model). A psychiatrist usually spends three years (subsequent to medical training) working under supervision in a hospital or a mental health clinic. The psychiatrist who chooses to be board certified must spend an additional two years working within the specialty of psychiatry before taking a set of grueling written and oral examinations. It should be noted that any physician can legally be referred to as a psychiatrist; therefore, the patient must investigate the credentials of the psychiatrist. Pertinent questions concern the institution of medical training, place and length of residency, and board certification. Most psychiatrists would not be offended by these questions, and those who are highly qualified usually enjoy the opportunity to answer them. If a psychiatrist is annoyed by the questions, it may be advisable to consult another therapist.

A *psychoanalyst* is usually, but not always, a psychiatrist; however, most psychiatrists are not psychoanalysts. A psychoanalyst usually bases his or her practice on Freudian theory (i.e., psychoanalysis). Training for psychoanalysts usually consists of years of intensive study and self-analysis. Psychoanalysts maintain that they are more prepared to help people with problems after studying mental processes in themselves. Although psychoanalysts are highly trained and skilled experts, psychoanalysis is usually not the most practical or parsimonious treatment for childhood psychological disorders.

Psychologists are professionals who have obtained considerable graduate training in the study of behavior. If the psychologist is referred to as doctor, this signifies that he or she possesses a Ph.D. degree. Other psychologists generally hold a M.A. or M.S. degree. The clinical psychologist is an expert, by virtue of training and experience, in abnormal behavior. Clinical psychologists usually spend four years in graduate study concentrating on theory, testing, and research dealing with abnormal behavior. A one-year internship in a mental institution or mental health clinic is required for the Ph.D. There are psychologists who specialize in other areas of psychology (e.g., educational, counseling, and developmental psychology); one of these professionals may act as the primary therapist for the child. This decision would depend on the nature of the disorder and, to some extent, on the availability of psychologists in a particular geographic area. Regardless of the area of specialization, the psychologist should be licensed by the state licensing board or should be closely supervised by a licensed psychologist. Psychologists do not have medical training; therefore, they may not prescribe medication. However, psychologists have highly specialized skills, exclusive to the profession, that are often essential in the treatment of a psychological disorder.

Social workers are found in many mental health settings. The social worker has generally completed a two-year course of study resulting in an M.S.W. degree. Much of the social work curriculum parallels that of the psychologist, without the emphasis on testing and research. The social worker usually establishes close personal relationships with clients (patients) and often works toward helping solve practical problems. These may include problems with transportation, housing, and medical expenses. Social workers should have extensive knowledge of the resources available in the community. One of the main functions of the social worker is to serve as a link between the client and other human service agencies within the community. Like the psychologist, in most states, the social worker should be licensed. Social workers with a M.S.W. from a certified school are eligible to join the Academy of Certified Social Workers after two years of experience under the supervision of a certified social worker.

The *psychiatric nurse* holds the R.N. degree and usually has had specialized training in a mental health facility. Psychiatric nurses work very closely with physicians and are often intensely involved with the patient (client). Nurses may administer but not prescribe medical treatment. Their recommendations are considered vital to effective treatment by other professionals.

Remember that physicians other than psychiatrists also play major roles in the treatment of psychological disorders of childhood. The expertise of family practitioners, neurologists, ophthamologists, pediatricians, internists, and other medical specialists is necessary in many instances.

Paraprofessional treatment is on the upswing. *Paraprofessionals* do not have graduate training in a mental health field. These people are primarily employed to increase human contact in inpatient (hospital) settings. Paraprofessionals are especially useful to children who have been placed in residential treatment facilities. Of particular value is the paraprofessional's ability to discuss the child's disorder with family members in lay terms. Paraprofessionals also assist professionals in carrying out a treatment plan.

The ideal treatment setting is one that combines the expertise of all of the mental health professionals. Multidisciplinary teams are available in many parts of the country. In situations where teams are not in use, experts should recognize the strengths of other professions and refer to them without hesitation.

WHERE TO FIND PEOPLE WHO CAN HELP

After examining the appropriateness of the referral and deciding on the type of professional who may be able to help, it is necessary to find these professionals. One method of reaching a professional is to look for *Social Service Organizations* in the yellow pages of the telephone book. Community mental health centers, child guidance clinics, and social workers are listed in this column. The cities in the United States that are covered by public mental health services are listed in Appendix I. Psychiatrists are listed under *Physicians and Surgeons,* and psychologists are listed as *Psychologists* and, sometimes, as *Marriage and Family Counselors.* The National Association for Mental Health (NAMH) is a citizen and consumer's group that maintains branch offices in most areas of the country. Addresses of local NAMH organizations are presented in Appendix II. The NAMH will supply a comprehensive directory of services upon request. Furthermore, directories of mental health services are offered by the National Institute of Mental Health (c/o Government Printing Office, Washington, D.C. 20402; cost: $7.00) and the National Society for Autistic Children (169 Tampa Avenue, Albany, N.Y. 12208). The addresses of other sources that provide extremely helpful information concerning mental health services are listed in Appendices III, IV, and V.

Community mental health centers are presently accessible to more than half the population. Funds for the initiation of these centers have been largely supplied by the federal government with the idea that mental health centers will eventually achieve economic independence. Unfortunately, this is an unrealistic goal for many centers, particularly those in poverty-stricken areas of the Southeast. Superior services are available in many mental health centers, and the multidisciplinary approach is usually implemented. Yet the quality of professional service varies drastically from one mental health center to the next. Standardized certification procedures now being used should eventually ensure uniform quality of service.

All children who need help have the right to treatment. Plans have been made to provide government-sponsored mental health programs that are accessible to every citizen. However, services are not available for many people who need them. Parents with handicapped children have a number of avenues in their goal of obtaining assistance. Again, these alternatives are thoroughly explored in *You Are Not Alone.*

COST

Probably the major consumer concern is the cost of mental health services. Although there is some variability, most private psychiatrists and psychologists charge approximately forty dollars an hour. At the rate of one or two hours per week for several weeks, private treatment can be an expensive proposition. Many therapists will arrange modifications in fee based on ability to pay. Scaled fees based on income is the general practice of public agencies like community mental health centers and federally funded child guidance clinics. Most of these agencies provide services for anyone in need, regardless of the individual's ability to pay.

Should the child require a residential treatment program, the consumer can generally expect exhorbitant prices in private care facilities. The widely acclaimed Brown Schools, residential treatment facilities for children with various disorders, charge approximately one thousand dollars a month. Very few people can afford this type of care. Public residential placement for children with severe psychological disorders is inadequate in most states and virtually nonexistent in others. State programs offer financial assistance to families who must seek private care because of the lack of public alternatives.

THE FIRST VISIT

The first visit to a mental health treatment center (public or private) usually includes an *intake interview.* The intake interview is used to obtain relevant information about the child and his or her family. The therapist or intake worker will probably ask not only about the problem but also about social history, health history, previous mental health contacts, developmental history, discipline patterns, and alcohol and drug use in the home. This information is necessary to a variety of treatment decisions.

Other topics, such as cost and confidentiality, should be discussed in detail during the initial contact. This is also a good opportunity for the client to form an impression regarding the desirability of the therapist. (However, in some agencies, the intake worker merely collects the data, and the client does not see the therapist until the second visit.) The client should carefully explain the problem and the desired objectives of treatment. The details of the treatment plan should be discussed with the client. The client should be told the expected length and the methods of treatment, as well as the probable outcome of the therapy.

THE TREATMENT PLAN

Treatment philosophies and approaches vary widely among mental health professionals. Yet certain elements should exist in any therapeutic mileu. There should be an atmosphere of respect. Respect for the individual is best demonstrated through nonjudgmental, sincere communication. Honesty is an integral part of the therapeutic environment. The client should expect empathy — but not sympathy — during the course of treatment. Empathy is simply the ability of a person to understand and feel from the perspective of another individual.

Actual therapy may take one or more of several forms. Individual play therapy, group therapy with peers, family counseling, parent education, and behavior modification are some commonly used approaches. It is important that adults responsible for the child play a vital, if not primary, role in the child's treatment. Adults who spend considerable time with the child are obviously in the best position to institute changes. It is unrealistic to expect significant improvement without the extensive involvement of parents and teachers.

Chapter **9**

NOTES
ON CHILD MANAGEMENT

Throughout the past quarter century, psychologists have developed effective principles of managing child behavior. Highly sophisticated procedures are required to control the more difficult behavior problems. Some general guidelines that can be applied to all children in most situations follow.

Learn to view a child's behavior in terms of specific responses that you can count.

Broad labels, such as aggressive, withdrawn, or overanxious, are not useful in developing a program to change behavior. It is helpful to specify problem behavior by observing that Bob hit Samuel three times during recess. This approach enables the parent or teacher to apply the appropriate consequences to specific responses. This is clearly the most efficient method of changing behavior.

Reward desirable behavior and ignore undesirable behavior.
We all know that behavior which is rewarded or reinforced is more likely to occur in the future. Children will respond to positive incentives (reinforcers) such as food, attention, praise, money, tokens, and toys. The procedure of administering these reinforcers immediately after the child's desirable behavior is called *positive reinforcement*. Reinforcement should be used often and applied to the child's achievement of small steps toward his or her goal. The teacher or parent can gradually require more work for the same reinforcers. Effective reinforcers vary with individuals. Some children respond better to praise and attention, whereas concrete rewards, such as raisins or tokens that can be exchanged for candy, may be more effective for others. The adult must determine the most effective reinforcer through trial and error.

Ignoring behavior is a powerful technique for eliminating undesirable behavior. Simply walking away is an effective response to a child's whining or temper tantrum. It is important to avoid eye contact or verbal exchange after an undesirable behavior.

Another more elaborate form of ignoring a child's behavior is to isolate the child in *time out*. This is a highly effective technique in which a child is placed in a small, well-lighted and ventilated room for several minutes following the undesirable behavior. A rule of thumb is to leave the child for one minute for each year of age; for example, an eight-year-old should stay in time out for eight minutes. The room should be devoid of attractions such as toys, books, or record players.

Generally, physical punishment is an ineffective, inefficient approach to discipline. First, physical punishment is only effective when the child is in the presence of the punishing agent (teacher or parent). Most children return to the same activity when the teacher or parent is not in the immediate environment. Second, physical punishment only temporarily suppresses the undesirable response. If the incentive (e.g., attention, praise from peers) remains, the behavior is likely to recur. Third, physical punishment may produce unpredictable behavior because of the negative emotion that is created. The child usually responds with anger, which may motivate him or her to retaliate in passive ways (e.g., forgetting to deliver Mom's message that she needs the car today). Fourth, children learn by example. Physical punishment therefore teaches the child to control others by physical aggression. Finally, most adults perceive a spanking or a scolding as punishment. However, the parent or teacher may be inadventently reinforcing the behavior with a spanking. Any form of attention (even negative kinds) may be highly rewarding to some children. For these reasons, physical punishment should generally be avoided, yet it can be usefully applied when a child's behavior creates danger (e.g., playing with matches or crossing the street without permission).

Be consistent in your child's discipline.

This is an extremely important guideline in approaching your child's behavior. Inconsistent discipline patterns usually produce confusion, anxiety, and undesirable behavior. Inconsistent discipline can be avoided through discussing both behavior patterns and the consequences that will be invoked for unacceptable behavior. Parents should also communicate with grandparents, babysitters, other siblings, and teachers about treatment of the child's behavior. It is vitally important to avoid threats that will not be carried out. Define acceptable behavior to the child and clearly explain the consequences of both acceptable and unacceptable behavior. It is more effective to demand desirable behavior than to correct undesirable behavior. Again, the parent and teacher should have clear ideas as to what behaviors are acceptable and unacceptable, and then they should apply consistent consequences to these behaviors.

Encourage independence and responsibility.

This important guideline has been espoused by Dr. Robert Lesowitz in his book, *Rules For Raising Kids.* Dr. Lesowitz points out that many young people fail to adjust to their freshman year at college. He largely attributes this failure to the lack of freedom to make important decisions coupled with the responsibility expected of these people during childhood and adolescence. Indeed, a child whose parents deny his or her independence in such matters as choosing clothing, setting routine study time, selecting friends, or earning money may have a difficult adjustment period after leaving home. On the other hand, a child to whom freedom without responsibility is granted may experience an even more difficult adjustment. Children should gradually be encouraged to be independent in such areas as cleanliness, grooming, assuming household chores, and successfully completing schoolwork. This freedom and responsibility pattern should continue until self-sufficiency is achieved—by late adolescence or early adulthood.

Encourage success experiences

One of the most important aspects of development is a child's self-concept. This refers to how a child views his or her self, and this information is obtained from other people and from the physical environment. If a child feels successful, his or her self-concept is usually positive. Success can be encouraged by providing activities within the child's range of ability. Children should generally be allowed to set their own goals. Children usually choose goals that are neither too easy nor too difficult to attain. Arbitrary standards for success and failure should be avoided. In his book, *Schools Without Failure*, Dr. William Glasser asserts that many of our children develop poor self-concepts because of failure experiences in school. He attributes much of the absenteeism, dropping out of school, delinquency, and general incompetence to unnecessary failure experiences that occur early in school. Dr. Glasser's concern about early failure experiences may be applied to the child in all spheres of life. A sense of competence, self-worth, and confidence can be instilled only through a success-oriented approach based on positive rather than on aversive contingencies.

Teach children by example.

Psychologists have studied the process of modeling and have concluded that children behave in a similar manner to others in the immediate environment. Not only will children model specific responses, they will model general behavior patterns. For example, children with two parents who smoke cigarettes are twice as likely to smoke. Children of parents who do not drink alcohol (no appropriate model for drinking) and children of alcoholic parents (inappropriate models) are more likely to be alcoholics than children whose parents drink in moderation. Parents and teachers may observe periods of rebellion in which the child rejects the adult model. These periods are usually an expression of independence and often dissipate if ignored. Children are quite perceptive in detecting discrepancies between the adult's stated views and the adult's behavior. This hyprocrisy is rejected, and the adult's behavior becomes a destructive influence on the child.

When in doubt, seek professional help.

The parental role is one of the most demanding, responsible roles in any society. This is also the role for which we are least prepared by formal education. Most parents rely on tradition and common sense in rearing their children. Frequently, parents may be unwittingly defeating their goals of providing the best parenting for their children. Most qualified psychologists, psychiatrists, and social workers have received a great deal of training in managing problem behaviors. Many of these professionals charge reasonable prices based on ability to pay. Therefore, parents and teachers should seek professional help when psychological or behavioral problems are observed.

These guidelines for child management are by no means exhaustive of the principles involved in competent parenting. Yet, the reader should have acquired useful information regarding the recognition and management of children with psychological disorders.

REFERENCES
AND SUGGESTED READINGS

American Psychiatric Association. *Diagnostic and Statistical Manual of Mental Disorders.* Second Edition. Washington, D.C.: American Psychiatric Association, 1968.

ANTHONY, S. *The Discovery of Death in Childhood and After.* Baltimore: Penguin Books, 1971.

BANDWIN, A. *Aggression: A Social Learning Analysis.* Englewood Cliffs, N.J.: Prentice-Hall, 1973.

―――― *Principles of Behavior Modification.* New York: Holt, Rinehart and Winston, 1969.

BAROFF, G. *Mental Retardation: Nature, Cause, and Management.* New York: Wiley, 1974.

BOWLBY, J. *Separation.* London: Penguin Books, 1971.

CHURCHILL, D., ALPERN, G., AND DE MYER, M., eds. *Infantile Autism.* Springfield, Illinois: Thomas, 1971.

CLEGG, A., AND MEGSON, B. *Children in Distress.* Baltimore: Penguin Books, 1968.

COLEMAN, MARY, ed. *The Autistic Syndromes.* Amsterdam: North Holland Publishing Company, 1976.

COPELAND, J. *For the Love of Ann.* New York: Ballantine Books, 1973.

DAVIE, R., BUTLER, N., AND GOLDSTEIN, H. *From Birth to Seven.* London: Longman, 1972.

DOUGALS, J. "Early disturbing events and later enuresis." In I. Kolvin, R. MacKeith, and S. Meadow, eds. *Bladder Control and Enuresis.* Philadelphia: Lippincott, 1973.

EHRMAN, L., OMENN, G., AND CASPARI, F., eds. *Genetics, Environment and Behavior: Implication for Educational Policy.* New York: Academic Press, 1972.

EVERARD, M., ed. *An Approach to Teaching Autistic Children.* Oxford: Pergamon Press, 1976.

GLASSER, W. *Schools Without Failure.* New York: Harper & Row, 1969.

GOLD, P. *Please Don't Say Hello.* New York: Human Sciences Press, 1975.

GREENFELD, J. *A Child Called Noah.* New York: Holt, Rinehart and Winston, 1972.

GROSSMAN, H., ed. *Manual on Terminology and Classification in Mental Retardation, 1973 Revision.* Washington, D.C.: American Association on Mental Deficiency, 1973.

HEBER, R. *Epidemiology of Mental Retardation.* Springfield, Ill.: Thomas, 1970.

INGRAM, T. "The classification of speech and language disorders in young children." In M. Rutler and J. Martin, eds. *The Child With Delayed Speech.* Philadelphia: Lippincott, 1972.

KAGAN, J., AND MOSS, H. *Birth to Maturity*. New York: Wiley, 1962.

KENNEDY, W. *Child Psychology*. Englewood Cliffs, N.J.: Prentice-Hall, 1971.

LOVASS, I. *The Autistic Child: Language Development Through Behavior Modification*. New York: Irvington Publishers, 1976.

MARTIN, G., AND PEAR, J. *Behavior Modification: What It Is and How To Do It*. Englewood Cliffs, N.J.: Prentice-Hall, 1978.

MENKES, J. *Textbook of Child Neurology*. Philadelphia: Lea and Fibiger, 1975.

MORLEY, M. *The Development and Disorders of Speech in Childhood*. Baltimore: Williams and Wilkins, 1965.

PARK, C. *The Siege*. New York: Harcourt Brace Jovanovich, 1967.

————, and SHAPIRO, L. *You Are Not Alone*. Boston: Little, Brown, 1976.

PIEPER, E. *Sticks and Stones*. New York: Human Policy Press, 1977.

RIMLAND, BERNARD. *Infantile Autism: The Syndrome and Its Implications for a Neural Theory of Behavior*. Englewood Cliffs, N.J.: Prentice-Hall, 1964.

RINN, R., AND MARKLE, A. *Positive Parenting*. Cambridge, Mass.: Research Media, Inc., 1977.

RITVO, BERNARD, *Autism: Diagnosis, Current Research and Management*. New York: Spectrum Publications, Inc., 1976.

ROBINSON, N., AND ROBINSON, H. *The Mentally Retarded Child*. New York: McGraw-Hill, 1976.

RUTTER, M., GRAHAM, D., AND YULE. W. *A Neuropsychiatric Study in Childhood.* Philadelphia: Lippincott, 1970.

SCHOPLER, E., AND REICHLER, R. *Psychopathology and Child Development: Research and Treatment.* New York: Plenum, 1976.

SCHULONAN, J., KASPER, J., AND THRONE, F. *Brain Damage and Behaviors.* Springfield, Ill.: Thomas, 1965.

STEWART, M., AND OLDS, S. *Raising a Hyperactive Child.* New York: Harper & Row, 1973.

STEWART, M. AND GATH, A. *Psychological Disorders of Children: A Handbook for Primary Care Physicians.* Baltimore: Williams and Wilkins, 1978.

THOMAS, A., CHESS, S., AND BIRCH, H. *Temperament and Behavior Disorders in Children.* New York: New York University Press, 1968.

WATSON, L. *Child Behavior Modification.* New York: Pergamon Press, 1973.

_____ *Behavior Modification of Mentally Retarded and Autistic Children: A Manual for Nurses, Teachers, and Parents.* New York: Pergamon Press, 1973.

WHITE, R. *The Special Child: A Parents' Guide to Mental Disabilities.* Boston: Little, Brown, 1978.

WING, L. *Autistic Children: A Guide for Parents and Professionals.* New York: Brunner/Mazel, 1972.

U.S. CITIES
HAVING PUBLIC
MENTAL HEALTH PROGRAMS

Alabama

Abbeville
Albertville
Alexander City
Andalusia
Anniston
Ashville
Athens
Atmore
Bay Minette
Birmingham
Brewton
Butler
Calera
Camden
Centre

Chatom
Clanton
Columbiana
Cullman
Dadeville
Decatur
Demopolis
Dothan
Elba
Enterprise
Eufaula
Eutaw
Evergreen
Fairhope
Fayette
Flat Rock
Florence

Foley
Fort Payne
Gadsden
Geneva
Georgiana
Goodwater
Greensboro
Greenville
Grove Hill
Guntersville
Haleyville
Hamilton
Hartselle
Haynesville
Helfin
Huntsville
Jacksonville
Jasper
Lineville
Livingston
Luverne
Marion
Mobile
Monroeville
Montgomery
Moulton
Mount Vernon
Oneonta
Opp
Ozark
Pell City
Phenix City
Pratteville
Robertsdale
Rockford
Russellville

Scottsboro
Selma
Shawmut
Siluria
Sylacauga
Talladega
Troy
Tuscaloosa
Tuskegee
Union Springs
Uniontown
University
Vernon
Wadley
Wetumpka
York

Alaska

Anchorage
Barrow
Bethel
Fairbanks
Homer
Juneau
Ketchikan
Kodiak
Kotzebue
Nome
Seward
Sitka

Arizona

Ajo
Apache Junction

Avondale
Benson
Bisbee
Bullhead City
Camp Verde
Casa Grande
Chandler
Clifton
Cottonwood
Douglas
El Mirage
Flagstaff
Glendale
Globe
Holbrook
Kingman
Lake Havasu City
Mesa
Nogales
Page
Peach Springs
Phoenix
Prescott
Safford
Scottsdale
Sedona
Show Low
Sierra Vista
Somerton
Springerville
St. Johns
Tempe
Tucson
Wellton
Whiteriver
Willcox

Winslow
Yuma

Arkansas

Arkadelphia
Ash Flat
Augusta
Batesville
Benton
Bentonville
Berryville
Brinkley
Camden
Clarksville
Clinton
Conway
Cotter
Crossett
Danville
Dermott
Des Arc
Dumas
El Dorado
Forrest City
Fort Smith
Harrison
Heber Springs
Helena
Hot Springs National Park
Huntsville
Jacksonville
Jasper
Jonesboro
Little Rock
Lonoke

Magnolia

Malvern

Marianna

Marshall

McCrory

McGehee

Melbourne

Mena

Monticello

Morrilton

Mount Ida

Mountain Home

Mountain View

Newport

North Little Rock

Ozark

Paris

Pine Bluff

Rison

Russellville

Salem

Scott

Searcy

Sheridan

Springdale

Star City

Stuttgart

Van Burden

Waldron

West Memphis

Wynne

California

Alameda

Altadena

Alturas

Anaheim

Antioch

Arcadia

Arroyo Grande

Atascadero

Auburn

Avenal

Bakersfield

Barstow

Beaumont

Belmont

Belvedere-Tiburon

Benicia

Berkeley

Brawley

Brea

Broderick

Buena Park

Burbank

Burlingame

Burney

Calabasas

Camarillo

Campbell

Canoga Park

Carmel

Carmichael

Carpinteria

Carson

Castro Valley

Ceres

Cerritos

Chester

Chico

China Lake

Chino
Chowchilla
Chula Vista
Clearlake Highlands
Coachella
Colusa
Compton
Concord
Corcoran
Corona
Costa Mesa
Covina
Crescent City
Crestline
Culver City
Daly City
Dana Point
Danville
Davis
Deer Park
Delano
Dinuba
Dixon
Dorris
Downieville
Earlimart
El Cajon
El Centro
El Monte
Elsinore
Encinitas
Encino
Escondido
Etna
Eureka
Fairfield

Fontana
Fort Bragg
Fountain Valley
French Camp
Fremont
Fresno
Fullerton
Garberville
Gardena
Gilroy
Glendale
Glendora
Goleta
Gonzales
Greenbrae
Greenfield
Half Moon Bay
Hanford
Happy Camp
Hawaiian Gardens
Hawthorne
Hayward
Hemet
Hollister
Huntington Beach
Imola
Indio
Inglewood
Kentfield
King City
Kings Beach
La Verne
La Habra
Laguna Beach
Laguna Hills
Lake View Terrace

Lakeport
Lakeside
Lancaster
Lawndale
Lindsay
Lodi
Loma Linda
Lompoc
Long Beach
Los Angeles
Los Banos
Los Gatos
Loyalton
Lynwood
Madera
Mariposa
Martinez
Menlo Park
Merced
Mill Valley
Millbrae
Mission Viejo
Modesto
Monrovia
Monterey
Mount Shasta
Mountain View
Napa
National City
Newhall
Newport Beach
North Hollywood
Northridge
Norwalk
Novato
Oakdale
Oakhurst

Oakland
Oceanside
Ontario
Orange
Oxnard
Pacifica
Pacoima
Palm Springs
Palo Alto
Pasadena
Paso Robles
Patterson
Patton
Perris
Petaluma
Philo
Pittsburg
Placerville
Pleasant Hill
Pleasanton
Point Reyes Station
Pomona
Porterville
Portola
Quincy
Ramona
Red Bluff
Redding
Redlands
Redondo Beach
Redwood City
Reedley
Richmond
Ridgecrest
Rio Vista
Riverside
Rosemead

Roseville
Ross
Sacramento
Salinas
San Anselmo
San Bernardino
San Bruno
San Clemente
San Diego
San Dimas
San Fernando
San Francisco
San Jose
San Leandro
San Luis Obispo
San Martin
San Mateo
San Pedro
San Rafael
Santa Ana
Santa Barbara
Santa Cruz
Santa Maria
Santa Monica
Santa Rosa
Santee
Seaside
Sebastopol
Simi Valley
Solvang
Sonoma
Sonara
South San Francisco
St. Helena
Stanford
Stockton
Sun Valley

Sunland
Sunnyvale
Sylmar
Tarzana
Thousand Oaks
Torrance
Tulare
Turlock
Ukiah
Upland
Vacaville
Vallejo
Van Nuys
Ventura
Victorville
Visalia
Vista
Walnut Creek
Watsonville
Weaverville
Westminster
Whittier
Willits
Willows
Woodland
Woodland Hills
Yosemite National Park
Yreka
Yuba City
Yucaipa

Colorado

Alamosa
Antonito
Arvada

Aurora
Boulder
Brighton
Broomfield
Burlington
Canon City
Castle Rock
Center
Cheyenne Wells
Colorado Springs
Commerce City
Cortez
Del Norte
Delta
Denver
Durango
Englewood
Evergreen
Flagler
Fort Collins
Fort Garland
Fort Lupton
Fort Morgan
Glenwood Springs
Golden
Granby
Grand Junction
Greeley
Green Mountain Falls
Gunnison
Hugo
Ignacio
Kiowa
La Jara
La Junta
LaFayette
Lakewood
Lamar

Larkspur
Leadville
Limon
Littleton
Longmont
Loveland
Monte Vista
Montrose
Northglenn
Nucla
Pagosa Springs
Pueblo
Saguache
Salida
San Luis
Sheridan
Simla
Steamboat Springs
Sterling
Telluride
Trinidad
Walsenburg
Westcliffe
Westminster
Yuma

Connecticut

Bridgeport
Bristol
Danbury
Deep River
Derby
Enfield
Essex
Farmington
Groton
Hamden

Hartford
Lakeville
Litchfield
Madison
Manchester
Meriden
Middletown
Milford
New Britain
New Canaan
New Haven
New London
New Milford
Newington
Newtown
Norwalk
Norwich
Plainville
Portland
Putnam
South Norwalk
Stamford
Torrington
Wallingford
Washington
Waterbury
Waterford
West Haven
Westport
Willimantic
Winsted

Delaware

Bridgeville
Delaware City
Dover
Georgetown

Laurel
Lewes
Middletown
New Castle
Newark
Roxanna
Wilmington

District of Columbia

Chevy Chase
Washington

Florida

Altamonte Springs
Apalachicola
Arcadia
Bartow
Belle Glade
Boca Ratan
Bonifay
Bradenton
Branford
Bristol
Bronson
Brooksville
Callahan
Century
Chattahoochee
Clearwater
Clermont
Cocoa Beach
Coconut Grove
Coral Gables
Crawfordville
Crestview
Cross City

Dade City
Davie
Daytona Beach
Defuniak Springs
Deland
Delray Beach
Deltona
Dunedin
Eustis
Fernandina Beach
Fort Lauderdale
Fort Myers
Fort Pierce
Fort Walton Beach
Fort White
Gainesville
Green Cove Springs
Greenwood
Hallandale
Hialeah
Hollywood
Homestead
Immokalee
Jacksonville
Jasper
Key West
Kissimmee
Lake Butler
Lake City
Lake Wales
Lake Worth
Lakeland
Largo
Lecanto
Leesburg
Live Oak

Mac Clenny
Madison
Marathon Shores
Mayo
Miami
Milton
Monticello
Naples
New Port Richey
New Smyrna Beach
North Miami
Ocala
Orange Park
Orlando
Palatka
Panama City
Pensacola
Perry
Pinellas Park
Plant City
Pompano Beach
Port St. Joe
Punta Gorda
Quincy
Riviera Beach
Rockledge
Sanford
Sarasota
Sebring
St. Augustine
St. Petersburg
Starke
Stuart
Sumterville
Tallahassee
Tampa

Tarpon Springs
Tavernier
Titusville
Trenton
Valparaiso
Venice
West Palm Beach
Winter Haven
Winter Park

Georgia

Adel
Albany
Alpharetta
Americus
Appling
Ashburn
Athens
Atlanta
Augusta
Austell
Bainbridge
Baxley
Blackshear
Blakely
Blue Ridge
Brunswick
Buchanan
Buckhead
Cairo
Calhoun
Camilla
Canton
Carrollton
Cartersville

Cedartown
Clyo
Colquitt
Columbus
Comer
Conyers
Cordele
Covington
Dallas
Dalton
Danielsville
Darien
Dawson
Decatur
Donaldsonville
Douglas
Douglasville
Dublin
East Point
Eastman
Elberton
Ellijay
Fitzgerald
Forest Park
Fort Oglethorpe
Fort Valley
Franklin
Gainesville
Gibson
Greensboro
Greenville
Griffin
Hinesville
Jasper
Jefferson
Jesup

Jonesboro
La Fayette
La Grange
Lakeland
Lawrenceville
Leesburg
Lincolnton
Louisville
Lyons
Macon
Madison
Manchester
Marietta
Metter
Milledgeville
Millen
Monroe
Morgan
Moultrie
Nashville
Newnan
Newton
Ocilla
Quitman
Reidsville
Riceboro
Riverdale
Roberta
Rome
Roswell
Savannah
Smyrna
Social Circle
Statenville
Statesboro
Summerville

Swainsboro
Sylvania
Sylvester
Thomasville
Thomson
Tifton
Toccoa
Trenton
Valdosta
Warner Robins
Warrenton
Washington
Waycross
Waynesboro
Winder
Woodbine

Hawaii

Aiea
Haleiwa
Hauula
Hilo
Honokaa
Honolulu
Kailua
Kaneohe
Kapaa
Kaunakakai
Keaau
Kealakekua
Kohala
Lahaina
Lanai City
Linue
Naalehu

Pahala
Pahoa
Pearl City
Puhi
Pukalani
Wahiawa
Wailuku
Waimanalo
Waimea
Waipahu

Idaho

American Falls
Blackfoot
Boise
Bonners Ferry
Burley
Caldwell
Coeur D' Alene
Council
Emmett
Gooding
Grangeville
Hailey
Idaho Falls
Kamiah
Kellogg
Lewiston
Malad
McCall
Montpelier
Moscow
Mountain Home
Nampa
Nez Perce

Orofino
Payette
Pocatello
Preston
Rexburg
Rupert
Salmon
Sandpoint
Soda Springs
St. Maries
Twin Falls
Weiser

Illinois

Addison
Albion
Alton
Anna
Arlington Heights
Aurora
Beardstown
Belleville
Belvidere
Bensenville
Berwyn
Bloomington
Breese
Burbank
Bushnell
Canton
Carbondale
Carrollton
Carthage
Cary
Centralia

Champaign	Hoopeston
Chester	Jacksonville
Chicago	Jerseyville
Chicago Heights	Joliet
Clinton	Kankakee
Crystal Lake	La Grange
Danville	Lacon
De Kalb	Lake Villa
Decatur	Lawrenceville
Des Plaines	Libertyville
Dixon	Macomb
East Moline	Manteno
East St. Louis	Marengo
Edwardsville	Marshall
Effingham	Mattoon
Elgin	Maywood
Elk Grove Village	McHenry
Evanston	McLeansboro
Evergreen Park	Metropolis
Fairfield	Moline
Fisher	Morris
Flora	Mount Carmel
Forest Park	Mount Sterling
Freeport	Mount Vernon
Galena	Moweaque
Galesburg	Murphysboro
Golconda	Newton
Granite City	Northfield
Grayslake	Oak Lawn
Hardin	Oak Park
Harvard	Olney
Harvey	Oregon
Herrin	Ottawa
Highland	Paris
Hines	Park Forest South
Hinsdale	Park Ridge

Peoria
Peru
Pittsfield
Pontiac
Princeton
Quincy
Red Bud
Robinson
Rochelle
Rock Island
Rockford
Romeoville
Rosiclare
Rushville
Salem.
Shelbyville
Skokie
Sparta
Spring Valley
Springfield
Stickney
Streator
Sullivan
Summit
Tinley Park
Toulon
Tuscola
Urbana
Vandalia
Vienna
Virginia
Waterloo
Watseka
Waukegan
West Frankfort
Westchester

Wheaton
Woodstock

Indiana

Anderson
Attica
Bedford
Bloomington
Bluffton
Boonville
Brazil
Brookville
Clinton
Columbia City
Columbus
Connersville
Corydon
Crawfordsville
Danville
Decatur
Dyer
East Chicago
Elkhart
English
Evansville
Fort Wayne
Frankfort
Gary
Goshen
Greencastle
Greenfield
Greensburg
Hammond
Hartford City
Highland

Huntington
Indianapolis
Jasper
Jeffersonville
Kendallville
Knox
Kokomo
La Porte
Lawrenceburg
Lebanon
Liberty
Logansport
Loogootee
Lyons
Madison
Marion
Martinsville
Michigan City
Middlebury
Mishawaka
Monticello
Mount Vernon
Muncie
Nashville
New Albany
New Castle
Noblesville
North Vernon
Paoli
Petersburg
Plymouth
Portland
Princeton
Rensselaer
Richmond
Rockport

Rockville
Salem
Seymour
Shelbyville
South Bend
Spencer
Sullivan
Tell City
Terre Haute
Tipton
Valparaiso
Versailles
Vevay
Vincennes
Wabash
Warsaw
Washington
West Lafayette
Westville
Whiting
Winchester

Iowa

Adel
Akron
Ames
Atlantic
Belmond
Bloomfield
Boone
Britt
Burlington
Cedar Rapids
Centerville
Chariton

Cherokee
Clarinda
Clinton
Corydon
Council Bluffs
Cresco
Davenport
Decorah
Denison
Des Moines
Dubuque
Elkader
Fairfield
Fort Dodge
Fort Madison
Grinnell
Ida Grove
Independence
Indianola
Iowa City
Jefferson
Keokuk
Knoxville
Le Mars
Maquoketa
Marengo
Marshalltown
Mason City
Mount Pleasant
New Hampton
Newton
Oakdale
Oelwein
Oskaloosa
Ottumwa
Sioux City

Spencer
Tipton
Wapello
Waterloo
Waukon
Waverly
West Union

Kansas

Anthony
Atchison
Augusta
Baldwin City
Baxter Springs
Belleville
Beloit
Bonner Springs
Clay Center
Coffeyville
Colby
Concordia
Council Grove
Desoto
Dodge City
El Dorado
Elkhart
Emporia
Eureka
Fort Scott
Garden City
Goodland
Great Bend
Greensburg
Halstead
Hays

Hiawatha
Hugoton
Humboldt
Hutchinson
Independence
Junction City
Kansas City
Kingman
Larned
Lawrence
Leavenworth
Liberal
Lyndon
Lyons
Manhattan
Mankato
Marion
Marysville
McPherson
Meade
Medicine Lodge
Merriam
Mission
Newton
Norton
Olathe
Osawatomie
Ottawa
Parsons
Phillipsburg
Pittsburg
Pratt
Salina
Satanta
Scott City
Shawnee Mission

St. John
Strong City
Topeka
Ulysses
Wamego
Washington
Wellington
Wichita

Kentucky

Albany
Anchorage
Arlington
Ashland
Augusta
Barbourville
Bardstown
Beattyville
Bedford
Benham
Benton
Berea
Booneville
Bowling Green
Brandenburg
Brinkley
Brooksville
Burkesville
Burlington
Cadiz
Campbellsville
Campton
Carlisle
Carrollton
Central City

Clinton	Jeremiah
Columbia	Kona
Corbin	La Grange
Covington	Lancaster
Cynthiana	Lawrenceburg
Danville	Lebanon
Dayton	Leitchefield
Elizabethtown	Lexington
Elkton	Liberty
Erlanger	London
Falmouth	Lothair
Flemingsburg	Louisa
Florence	Louisville
Fort Mitchell	Lynch
Fort Thomas	Madisonville
Frankfort	Manchester
Frenchburg	Marion
Fulton	Mayfield
Georgetown	Maysville
Grayson	McKee
Greensburg	Monticello
Greenup	Morehead
Greenville	Mount Olivet
Hardinsburg	Mount Sterling
Harlan	Mount Vernon
Harrodsburg	Murray
Hazard	New Castle
Hindman	Newport
Hodgenville	Nicholasville
Hopkinsville	Owensboro
Hyden	Owenton
Inez	Owingsville
Irvine	Paducah
Jackson	Paintsville
Jamestown	Paris
Jeffersontown	Pikeville

Pineville
Prestonsburg
Princeton
Radcliff
Richmond
Salyersville
Sandy Hook
Shelbyville
Shepherdsville
Somerset
South Williamson
Springfield
Stanford
Stanton
Stark
Taylorsville
Vanceburg
Versailles
West Liberty
Whitesburg
Whitley City
Wickliffe
Williamsburg
Williamstown
Winchester

Louisiana

Abbeville
Alexandria
Arcadia
Bastrop
Baton Rouge
Benton
Bogalusa
Bossier City

Bunkie
Chalmette
Clinton
Columbia
Cotton Valley
Coushatta
Covington
Crowley
De Ridder
Delhi
Donaldsonville
Dubach
Farmerville
Franklinton
Greenwood
Hammond
Hardwood
Harvey
Homer
Houma
Jackson
Jefferson
Jennings
Jonesboro
Jonesville
Keithville
Kinder
La Combe
Lafayette
Lake Charles
Lake Providence
Leesville
Mandeville
Mansfield
Many
Marksville

Metairie
Minden
Monroe
Natchitoches
New Iberia
New Orleans
New Roads
Norco
Oak Grove
Oakdale
Opelousas
Patterson
Pineville
Plain Dealing
Port Allen
Rayville
Ringgold
Ruston
Shreveport
Slidell
St. Joseph
St. Martinville
Sulphur
Tallulah
Vivian
West Monroe
Winnfield
Zachary

Maine

Augusta
Bangor
Bar Harbor
Bath
Belfast

Biddeford
Bingham
Boothbay Harbor
Bridgton
Brunswick
Damarescotta
Dover-Foxcroft
Easy Boothbay
East Machias
Ellsworth
Ellsworth Falls
Fort Fairfield
Fort Kent
Greene
Houlton
Lewiston
Lincoln
Millinocket
Norway
Portland
Presque Isle
Rockland
Rockport
Rumford
Saco
Sanford
Van Buren
Waterville
Wilton
York

Maryland

Annapolis
Baltimore
Bel Air

Berlin
Bethesda
Bladensburg
Cambridge
Capitol Heights
Catonsville
Centreville
Chestertown
Cheverly
Churchton
Cockeysville
College Park
Columbia
Crisfield
Crownsville
Cumberland
Denton
Dundalk
Easton
Elkton
Ellicott City
Federalsburg
Frederick
Frostburg
Gaithersburg
Glen Burnie
Glenelg
Grantsville
Hagerstown
Havre De Grace
Gyattsville
Jessup
La Plata
Lanham
Laurel
Lexington Park

Marlow Heights
Oakland
Odenton
Olney
Prince Frederick
Reisterstown
Rockville
Salisbury
Seat Pleasant
Severna Park
Silver Spring
Suitland
Sykesville
Takoma Park
Towson
Upper Marlboro
Westminster
Westover
Wheaton
Williamsport

Massachusetts

Amherst
Athol
Attleboro
Ayer
Baldwinville
Barre
Bellingham
Belmont
Berkley
Beverly
Boston
Bridgewater
Brighton

Brockton
Brookline
Burlington
Cambridge
Carlisle
Charlestown
Chatham
Chelsea
Chicopee
Clinton
Concord
Dedham
Dorchester
Duxbury
East Boston
East Bridgewater
East Taunton
Edgartown
Fall River
Falmouth
Fitchburg
Framingham
Franklin
Gardner
Georgetown
Gloucester
Great Barrington
Greenfield
Hanover
Hathorne
Haverhill
Holyoke
Hopedale
Hyannis
Ipswich
Jamaica Plain

Lawrence
Lee
Leicester
Lexington
Lowell
Lynn
Lynnfield
Malden
Marlborough
Medfield
Melrose
Methuen
Middleboro
Milford
Needham
New Bedford
New Marlboro
Newburyport
Newton
Newton Centre
Newton Lower Falls
Norfolk
North Adams
North Brookfield
North Reading
Northampton
Norwood
Orange
Palmer
Peabody
Petersham
Pittsfield
Pocasset
Quincy
Raynham
Reading

Rehoboth
Revere
Roxbury
Rutland
Salem
Saugus
Scituate
Seekonk
Somerville
South Attleboro
South Boston
South Wellfleet
Southbridge
Springfield
Stockbridge
Stoneham
Stoughton
Swampscott
Taunton
Walpole
Waltham
Watertown
Webster
Wellesley
West Newton
Westboro
Westfield
Westwood
Whitinsville
Williamstown
Winchendon
Woburn
Worcester

Michigan

Adrian
Algonac

Alma
Alpena
Ann Arbor
Bad Axe
Battle Creek
Bay City
Belleville
Big Rapids
Birmingham
Brighton
Cadillac
Capac
Caro
Central Lake
Centreville
Charlotte
Cheboygan
Chelsea
Coldwater
Dearborn
Dearborn Heights
Detroit
Dimondale
Eloise
Escanaba
Farmington Hills
Ferndale
Flint
Frankfort
Garden City
Gaylord
Gladwin
Grand Haven
Grand Rapids
Grayling
Grosse Pointe Farms
Grosse Pointe Woods
Hancock

Harbor Beach
Harrison
Hart
Highland Park
Hillsdale
Holland
Houghton
Houghton Lake
Howell
Hudsonville
Inkster
Ionia
Iron Mountain
Iron River
Jackson
Kalamazoo
Kalkaska
Kinde
Lansing
Lapeer
Lincoln Park
Livonia
Manistique
Marine City
Marquette
Mason
Midland
Milan
Monroe
Mount Clemens
Mount Pleasant
Munising
Muskegon
Newberry
Northville
Oak Park
Owosso
Petoskey

Pigeon
Pontiac
Port Huron
Reed City
Rose City
Royal Oak
Saginaw
Saline
Sandusky
Sault Ste. Marie
Sebewaing
Southfield
St. Clair Shores
St. Ignace
St. Johns
St. Joseph
Standish
Stanton
Sterling Heights
Tawas City
Temperance
Traverse City
Troy
Ubly
Warren
West Bloomfield
White Cloud
White Pine
Whitmore Lake
Wyandotte
Wyoming
Yale
Ypsilanti

Minnesota

Alberta Lea
Alexandria

Anoka

Austin

Bagley

Baudette

Bemidji

Blue Earth

Braham

Brainerd

Breckenridge

Buffalo

Burnsville

Caledonia

Crookston

Detroit Lakes

Duluth

Elk River

Fairmont

Faribault

Fergus Falls

Gaylord

Glenwood

Grand Rapids

Hastings

Hibbing

Hutchinson

Jackson

La Crescent

Lake City

Le Center

Little Falls

Luverne

Mankato

Mantorville

Marshall

Melrose

Minneapolis

Minnetonka

Moorhead

Moose Lake

Morris

Mound

New Ulm

Northfield

Owatonna

Park Rapids

Pine River

Pipestone

Plainview

Preston

Red Wing

Rochester

Roseau

Shakopee

South St. Paul

Spring Grove

St. Cloud

St. James

St. Paul

St. Peter

Thief River Falls

Virginia

Wabasha

Waconia

Walker

Waseca

White Earth

Willmar

Windom

Winona

Woodbury

Worthington

Zumbrota

Mississippi

Aberdeen
Ackerman
Amory
Ashland
Batesville
Bay Spring
Bay St. Louis
Belzoni
Biloxi
Brandon
Brookhaven
Bruce
Calhoun City
Carrollton
Carthage
Charleston
Clarksdale
Cleveland
Clinton
Coffeeville
Collins
Columbus
De Kalb
Decatur
Eupora
Fayette
Forest
Fulton
Greenville
Greenwood
Grenada
Gulfport
Hattiesburg
Hernando

Holly Springs
Houston
Indianola
Jackson
Kosciusko
Laurel
Lexington
Liberty
Louisville
Macon
Marks
McComb
Meadville
Meridian
Monticello
Natchez
New Albany
Oakland
Oxford
Philadelphia
Picayune
Pontotoc
Poplarville
Purvis
Quitman
Raleigh
Rolling Fork
Senatobia
Southaven
Starkville
Sumner
Tunica
Tupelo
Tylertown
Vaiden
Water Valley

West Point
Whitfield
Wiggins
Winona
Woodville

Missouri

Albany
Blue Springs
Boonville
Buckner
California
Cameron
Cape Girardeau
Carrollton
Carthage
Centralia
Chillicothe
Clayton
Columbia
Crocker
Eldon
Farmington
Fayette
Florissant
Fredericktown
Fulton
Hannibal
Hayti
Hermann
Hillsboro
Independence
Joplin
Kansas City
Kennett
Keytesville

Kinlock
Kirksville
Lamar
Lebanon
Lee's Summit
Lexington
Liberty
Louisiana
Lutesville
Malden
Marshall
Maryville
Mexico
Moberly
Monroe City
Montgomery City
Neosho
Nevada
New Madrid
North Kansas City
Paris
Perryville
Pineville
Platte City
Raytown
Richmond
Rolla
Sedalia
Springfield
St. Charles
St. Joseph
St. Louis
Ste. Genevieve
Sullivan
Troy
Valley Park
Versailles

Warrensburg
Warrenton
Washington
Webster Groves

Montana

Anaconda
Ashland
Big Timber
Billings
Butte
Choteau
Colstrip
Columbus
Conrad
Cut Bank
Dillon
Forsyth
Glasgow
Glendive
Great Falls
Hamilton
Hardin
Harlowton
Havre
Helena
Kalispell
Lewistown
Libby
Livingston
Miles City
Missoula
Plentywood
Red Lodge
Ronan

Roundup
Shelby
Stanford
Thompson Falls
Warm Springs
Winnett

Nebraska

Alliance
Alma
Auburn
Beatrice
Beaver City
Benkelman
Blair
Bridgeport
Broken Bow
Cambridge
Central City
Chadron
Clay Center
Columbus
Crawford
Crete
Curtis
David City
Elwood
Fairbury
Falls City
Franklin
Fremont
Geneva
Gothenburg
Grand Island
Hastings

Hebron
Holdrege
Imperial
Kearney
Lexington
Lincoln
Loup City
McCook
Minden
Mullen
Nebraska City
Norfolk
North Platte
Ogallala
Omaha
Osceola
Pawnee City
Red Cloud
Scottsbluff
Seward
Sidney
Superior
Tecumseh
Wahoo
York

Nevada

Carson City
Elko
Ely
Fallon
Hawthorne
Henderson
Las Vegas
North Las Vegas

Reno
Sparks
Winnemucca
Yerington

New Hampshire

Berlin
Claremont
Colebrook
Concord
Conway
Dover
Exeter
Franklin
Hampstead
Hanover
Henniker
Hillsborough
Keene
Laconia
Lancaster
Littleton
Manchester
Nashua
New London
North Conway
Peterborough
Plymouth
Portsmouth
Rindge
Salem
Suncook
Tilton
Wolfeboro
Woodsville

New Jersey

Allentown
Asbury Park
Atlantic City
Basking Ridge
Bayonne
Belford
Belle Mead
Belleville
Belvidere
Berkeley Heights
Boonton
Bridgeton
Burlington
Camden
Cape May
Cedar Grove
Cherry Hill
Cranford
Denville
Dumont
Dunellen
East Brunswick
East Orange
Eatontown
Elizabeth
Englewood
Fair Lawn
Farmingdale
Flemington
Freehold
Greystone Park
Guttenberg
Hackensack
Hackettstown

Hammonton
Hazlet
Hoboken
Irvington
Jersey City
Kearny
Lakeland
Lakewood
Linden
Livingston
Long Branch
Lyndhurst
Manahawkin
Marlboro
Marlton
Metuchen
Middletown
Millburn
Millington
Millville
Montclair
Morristown
Mount Holly
Neptune
New Brunswick
New Lisbon
New Shrewsbury
Newark
Newton
Orange
Paramus
Park Ridge
Passaic
Paterson
Perth Amboy
Phillipsburg

Piscataway
Plainfield
Pompton Lakes
Pompton Plains
Princeton
Red Bank
Ridgefield Park
Ridgewood
Saddle Brook
Salem
Secaucus
Somerville
South Amboy
South Orange
Summit
Teaneck
Toms River
Trenton
Union City
Vineland
Voorhees Township
Waldwick
Wayne
Weehawken
West Collingswood
Wickatunk
Willingboro
Woodbury
Wyckoff

New Mexico

Alamogordo
Albuquerque
Artesia
Carlsbad

Clovis
Deming
Farmington
Gallup
Las Cruces
Las Vegas
Lordsburg
Raton
Ruidoso
Santa Fe
Silver City
Socorro
Truth or Consequences

New York

Albany
Albion
Alden
Amityville
Amsterdam
Angola
Astoria
Attica
Auburn
Babylon
Batavia
Bath
Bay Shore
Bayside
Beacon
Bellerose
Belmont
Bethpage
Binghamton
Boonville

Brentwood
Brewster
Bronx
Brooklyn
Buffalo
Burlingham
Burnt Hills
Cairo
Cambridge
Camden
Canandaigua
Canton
Carmel
Central Islip
Central Square
Central Valley
Churchville
Clifton Springs
Cohoes
Cold Spring
Commack
Conesville
Cooperstown
Copiague
Corning
Corona
Cortland
Dewitt
Dobbs Ferry
Douglaston
Dunkirk
East Aurora
East Meadow
East Rockaway
East Syracuse
Eastchester

Elizabethtown
Ellenville
Elmhurst
Elmira
Elmont
Endwell
Far Rockaway
Farmingville
Ferndale
Flushing
Forest Hills
Fort Plain
Franklin Square
Fredonia
Freeport
Freeville
Fulton
Garden City
Geneva
Glen Cove
Glen Oaks
Glens Falls
Goshen
Gouverneur
Greene
Hamburg
Hamilton
Harrison
Hauppauge
Haverstraw
Helmuth
Hempstead
Herkimer
Hicksville
Hornell
Howard Beach

Hudson

Hudson Falls

Huntington

Islip

Ithaca

Jackson Heights

Jamaica

Jamaica Estates

Jamestown

Johnson City

Johnstown

Katonah

Kew Gardens

Kings Park

Kingston

Lackawanna

Lake Grove

Lake Placid

Lake Ronkonkoma

Lancaster

Latham

Laurelton

Lawrence

Liberty

Little Falls

Lockport

Long Beach

Lowville

Lynbrook

Lyons

Lysander

Machias

Mahopac

Malone

Mamaroneck

Manhasset

Marcy

Massena

Mastic Beach

Melville

Middletown

Millbrook

Monticello

Mount Kisco

Mount Morris

Mount Vernon

Naples

New Hampton

New Hyde Park

New Paltz

New Rochelle

New York

Newburgh

Niagara Falls

North Collins

North Creek

North Syracuse

North Tarrytown

North Tonawanda

Norwich

Nyack

Oceanside

Ogdensburg

Olean

Oneida

Oneonta

Orangeburg

Ossining

Oswego

Ovid

Owego

Oyster Bay

Paradox
Patchogue
Peekskill
Penn Yan
Perry
Plainview
Plattsburgh
Pleasantville
Pomona
Port Chester
Port Jervis
Port Washington
Potsdam
Poughkeepsie
Pulaski
Queens Village
Randolph
Rego Park
Rhinebeck
Richmond Hill
Ridgewood
Riverhead
Rochester
Rockville Centre
Rome
Roosevelt
Roslyn
Roslyn Heights
Rye
Salamanca
Sands Point
Saranac Lake
Saratoga Springs
Saugerties
Schenectady
Schoharie

Seaford
Seneca Falls
Smithtown
Solvay
South Fallsburg
Spring Valley
Springville
Star Lake
Staten Island
Suffern
Syosset
Syracuse
Tarrytown
Ticonderoga
Tonawanda
Troy
Tuckahoe
Tupper Lake
Utica
Valhalla
Walton
Wampsville
Wantagh
Wards Island
Waterloo
Watertown
Watkins Glen
Wellsville
West Brentwood
West Seneca
Westbury
White Plains
Whitehall
Willard
Williamsville
Wingdale

Woodbury
Woodmere
Woodside
Wyandanch
Yonkers
Yorktown Heights

North Carolina

Ahoskie
Asheboro
Asheville
Ayden
Bakersville
Bayboro
Beaufort
Boone
Brevard
Bryson City
Buies Creek
Burgaw
Burlington
Burnsville
Butner
Camden
Chapel Hill
Charlotte
Cherryville
Clarkton
Clinton
Columbia
Concord
Cullowhee
Currituck
Dallas
Danbury

Dunn
Durham
Edenton
Elizabeth City
Elizabethtown
Elkin
Enfield
Fayetteville
Forest City
Gastonia
Goldsboro
Greensboro
Greenville
Hayesville
Hazelwood
Henderson
Hendersonville
Hertford
Hickory
High Point
Hillsborough
Jacksonville
Jefferson
Kenansville
Kinston
Laurinburg
Lenoir
Lexington
Lincolnton
Louisburg
Lumberton
Manteo
Marble
Marion
Marshall
Mocksville

Mooresville
Morehead City
Morganton
Mount Airy
Murfreesboro
New Bern
Newland
Oxford
Pinehurst
Pittsboro
Plymouth
Raeford
Raleigh
Roanoke Rapids
Rockingham
Rocky Mount
Rose Hill
Roxboro
Rutherfordton
Salisbury
Sanford
Scotland Neck
Shelby
Siler City
Smithfield
Snow Hill
Sparta
Spring Hope
Statesville
Supply
Swanquarter
Tarboro
Taylorsville
Trenton
Troy
Tryon

Wadesboro
Warrenton
Washington
Wentworth
Whiteville
Wilkesboro
Williamston
Wilmington
Wilson
Windsor
Winston-Salem
Woodland
Yadkinville
Yanceyville

North Dakota

Bismarck
Bowbells
Cavalier
Drake
Drayton
Fargo
Finley
Forman
Grafton
Grand Forks
Harvey
Hillsboro
Jamestown
Kenmare
Lakota
Lisbon
Mandan
Mayville
McVille

Minot
New Town
Oakes
Park River
Stanley
Villey City
Walhalla

Ohio

Akron
Alliance
Amsterdam
Ashland
Ashtabula
Athens
Barberton
Barnesville
Batavia
Bellefontaine
Bellevue
Berea
Bergholz
Bowling Green
Brunswick
Bucyrus
Burton
Cadiz
Cambridge
Canton
Carrollton
Celina
Chagrin Falls
Chardon
Chillicothe
Cincinnati

Cleveland
Coldwater
Columbus
Cuyahoga Falls
Dayton
Defiance
Delaware
Dover
East Liverpool
Eaton
Elyria
Englewood
Enon
Euclid
Fairborn
Findlay
Fostoria
Franklin
Fremont
Galion
Garfield Heights
Genoa
Georgetown
Germantown
Greenville
Grove City
Hamilton
Hillsboro
Ironton
Kent
Kenton
Kettering
Lakewood
Lancaster
Lebanon
Lima

Lisbon
Logan
London
Lorain
Mansfield
Marietta
Marion
Martins Ferry
Marysville
Massillon
McArthur
Medina
Mentor
Middletown
Millersburg
Mount Gilead
Mount Vernon
Nelsonville
New Carlisle
Newark
Newcomerstown
Northfield
Northwood
Norwalk
Oregon
Orrville
Ottawa
Painesville
Parma Heights
Paulding
Port Clinton
Portsmouth
Ravenna
Richwood
Rittman
Sandusky

Sebring
Sidney
Smithville
Springfield
St. Clairsville
St. Marys
Steubenville
Struthers
Tiffin
Tiltonsville
Toledo
Toronto
Trotwood
Troy
Uhrichsville
Upper Sandusky
Urbana
Van Wert
Wadsworth
Warren
Waverly
West Chester
West Union
Willard
Wilmington
Woodsfield
Wooster
Worthington
Xenia
Youngstown
Zanesville

Oklahoma

Ada
Altus

Ardmore
Arkansas City
Atoka
Bartlesville
Bethany
Bristow
Chickasha
Clinton
Coalgate
Cushing
Del City
Drumright
Duncan
Durant
Edmond
Enid
Eufaula
Fort Supply
Heavener
Holdenville
Hugo
Idabel
Lawton
Lindsay
McAlester
Mcloud
Midwest City
Moore
Muskogee
Norman
Oklahoma City
Okmulgee
Pauls Valley
Ponca City
Pryor
Purcell

Sallisaw
Sapulpa
Shawnee
Spencer
Stigler
Stillwater
Stilwell
Sulphur
Tahlequah
Talihina
Tishomingo
Tulsa
Vinita
Wagoner
Weatherford
Wheatland
Wilburton
Winfield
Woodward

Oregon

Albany
Astoria
Baker
Beaverton
Bend
Brookings
Burns
Coos Bay
Coquille
Corvallis
Dallas
Enterprise
Eugene
Fossil

Gladstone
Gold Beach
Grants Pass
John Day
Klamath Falls
La Grande
Lakeview
Lincoln City
Madras
Marylhurst
McMinnville
Medford
Newport
North Bend
Ontario
Oregon City
Pendleton
Portland
Prineville
Redmond
Roseburg
Salem
Seaside
St. Helens
The Dalles
Tillamook
Troutdale
Wilsonville

Pennsylvania

Abington
Albion
Aliquippa
Allentown
Altoona

Ambler
Ardmore
Beaver Falls
Bedford
Bellefonte
Bethel Park
Bethlehem
Braddock
Bradford
Bridgeville
Brookville
Broomall
Bryn Mawr
Butler
Camp Hill
Carbondale
Carlisle
Carnegie
Chalfont
Chambersburg
Chester
Clairton
Clarion
Clarks Summit
Clearfield
Coatesville
Coraopolis
Corry
Coudersport
Croydon
Danville
Darby
Devon
Downingtown
Doylestown
Du Bois

East Stroudsburg
Easton
Edinboro
Elizabeth
Elizabethville
Emporium
Erie
Farrell
Fort Washington
Forty Fort
Franklin
Fredericktown
Gettysburg
Glenolden
Greensburg
Greenville
Hanover
Harrisburg
Haverford
Havertown
Hazleton
Hershey
Hollsopple
Homestead
Honesdale
Houtzdale
Hunlock Creek
Huntingdon
Indiana
Johnstown
Jonestown
Kane
Kittanning
Lafayette Hill
Lake Silkworth
Lancaster

Lansdale
Latrobe
Lebanon
Lehighton
Lewisburg
Lewistown
McConnelsburg
McKees Rocks
McKeesport
Meadville
Media
Mifflintown
Milford
Millersburg
Monessen
Monroeville
Montrose
Mount Pleasant
Mount Union
Nanticoke
New Britain
New Castle
New Kensington
Norristown
North Braddock
North Charleroi
North East
Oil City
Penndel
Pennsburg
Philadelphia
Pittsburgh
Pittston
Port Allegany
Pottstown
Pottsville

Punxsutawney
Reading
Ridgway
Rochester
Royersford
Saxton
Sayre
Schellsburg
Scranton
Sellersville
Sewickley
Shamokin
Sharon
Smethport
Somerset
St. Marys
Steelton
Stroudsburg
Sunbury
Tarentum
Taylor
Titusville
Torrance
Towanda
Trevose
Tunkhannock
Turtle Creek
Tyrone
Union City
Uniontown
University Park
Upland
Verona
Warren
Washington
Waymart

Waynesburg
Wellsboro
Wernersville
West Chester
Wilkes-Barre
Wilkinsburg
Williamsport
Willow Grove
York

Rhode Island

Barrington
Charlestown
Chepachet
Cranston
Greenville
Newport
Pawtucket
Providence
Riverside
Warwick
Woonsocket

South Carolina

Aiken
Anderson
Barnwell
Beaufort
Bennettsville
Bishopville
Camden
Charleston
Chester
Chesterfield

Columbia

Conway

Denmark

Dillon

Easley

Florence

Gaffney

Georgetown

Greenville

Greenwood

Greer

Hartsville

Kingstree

Lake City

Lancaster

Laurens

Manning

Marion

Moncks Corner

Orangeburg

Pickens

Rock Hill

Seneca

Simpsonville

Spartanburg

St. Matthews

Summerville

Sumter

Travelers Rest

Union

York

South Dakota

Aberdeen

Armour

Beresford

Bonesteel

Brookings

Custer

De Smet

Flandreau

Gregory

Highmore

Hot Springs

Howard

Huron

Kadoka

Kennebec

Lemmon

Miller

Mission

Mitchell

Onida

Pierre

Presho

Rapid City

Sioux Falls

Spearfish

Sturgis

Wagner

Wall

Watertown

Wessington Springs

White River

Winner

Woonsocket

Yankton

Tennessee

Abingdon

Alamo
Ashland City
Athens
Bolivar
Bristol
Brownsville
Celina
Centerville
Chattanooga
Church Hill
Clarksville
Cleveland
Columbia
Cookeville
Copperhill
Covington
Crossville
Demascus
Decaturville
Dickson
Dover
Dyersburg
Elizabethton
Erin
Fayetteville
Franklin
Gallatin
Greenville
Harriman
Henderson
Hohenwald
Jackson
Johnson City
Kingsport
Knoxville
La Follette

Lawrenceburg
Lebanon
Lewisburg
Lexington
Linden
Louisville
Madison
Madisonville
Manchester
Martin
Maryville
McMinnville
Memphis
Morristown
Mountain City
Murfreesboro
Nashville
Oak Ridge
Oneida
Paris
Pulaski
Rogersville
Savannah
Selmer
Shelbyville
Smyrna
Sneedville
Springfield
Tiptonville
Trenton
Tullahoma
Union City
Waverly
Waynesboro
Western State Hospital
Winchester

Texas

Abilene
Alice
Amarillo
Anahuac
Andrews
Arlington
Athens
Austin
Bastrop
Bay City
Baytown
Beaumont
Beeville
Belton
Big Spring
Bowie
Breckenridge
Brownfield
Brownsville
Brownwood
Bryan
Burnet
Cameron
Canton
Center
Childress
Clarksville
Cleburne
Colorado City
Conroe
Corpus Christi
Corsicana
Crosbyton
Cuero

Dallas
De Queen
Decatur
Del Rio
Denison
Dumas
Eagle Pass
Edinburg
El Paso
Elsa
Falfurrias
Fort Davis
Fort Hood
Fort Worth
Fredericksburg
Freer
Gainesville
Galveston
Gonzales
Graham
Greenville
Groesbeck
Harlingen
Haskell
Hebbronville
Hempstead
Hereford
Hillsboro
Hope
Houston
Huntsville
Junction
Kerrville
Killeen
Kingsville
Kountze

Olympia
Othello
Pasco
Port Angeles
Port Townsend
Poulsbo
Pullman
Puyallup
Quincy
Renton
Republic
Richland
Ritzville
Seattle
Sedro Wooley
Shelton
Snoqualmie
South Bend
Spokane
Sprague
Stanwood
Sunnyside
Tacoma
Tonasket
Toppenish
Vancouver
Vashon Island
Walla Walla
Wenatchee
White Salmon
Yakima

West Virginia

Barboursville
Beckley

Lamesa
Lampasas
Laneville
Laredo
Levelland
Lewisville
Longview
Lubbock
Lufkin
Marlin
Marshall
McAllen
McKinney
Meridian
Mesquite
Midland
Mineral Wells
Monahans
Mount Pleasant
Nacogdoches
Nashville
New Boston
New Braunfels
Odessa
Orange
Paducah
Palestine
Pampa
Paris
Pasadena
Pecos
Plainview
Port Arthur
Port Lavaca
Post
Quanah

Quitman
Richardson
Richmond
Rio Grande City
Rusk
San Angelo
San Antonio
San Marcos
Seagraves
Seguin
Seymour
Sherman
Sinton
Snyder
Stamford
Stephenville
Sweetwater
Taylor
Temple
Terrell
Texarkana
Texas City
Tyler
Vernon
Victoria
Waco
Weslaco
Wharton
Wichita Falls
Zapata

Utah

Beaver
Bicknell
Blanding

Bluff
Brigham City
Castle Dale
Cedar City
Delta
Duchesne
Dugway
East Carbon City
Eureka
Farmington
Fillmore
Green River
Ibapah
Junction
Kanab
Kearns
Logan
Manti
Mexican Hat
Midvale
Moab
Montezuma Creek
Monticello
Murray
Nephi
Ogden
Panguitch
Park City
Price
Provo
Richfield
Riverton
Salt Lake City
Sandy
Spanish Fork
St. George

Tooele
Vernal
Wendover

Vermont

Bellows Falls
Bennington
Brattleboro
Burlington
Jeffersonville
Manchester
Monpelier
Newport
Rutland
South Burlington
St. Johnsbury
Waterbury
White River Junction

Virginia

Accomac
Alexandria
Amherst
Annandale
Appomattox
Arlington
Bedford
Berryville
Blacksburg
Bland
Bowling Green
Burkeville
Cape Charles
Catawba

Charlottesville
Chesterfield
Clifton Forge
Cross Junction
Danville
Emporia
Falls Church
Franklin
Fredericksburg
Front Royal
Galax
Grafton
Grundy
Hampton
Harrisonburg
Hillsville
Independence
Leesburg
Lexington
Louisa
Lovingston
Luray
Lynchburg
Manassas
Marion
Martinsville
McLean
Nassawadox
Newport News
Norfolk
Orange
Palmyra
Petersburg
Portsmouth
Providence Forge
Pulaski

S
S
V
V
W
W
Wa
Wil
Wir
Wis
Woo
Woo
Wyth

Washi

Aberd
Anaco
Auburr
Bayview
Bellevue
Bellingh

Blaine
Bremerton
Brewster
Carnation
Chehalis
Clarkston
Cle Elum
Colville
Connell
Coulee Da
Coupeville
Davenport
Dayton
Eastsound
Ellensburg
Elma
Ephrata
Everett
Fort Steil
Friday H
Goldend
Issaquah
Kenmor
Kirklan
La Con
Long B
Longvie
Lopez
Lynde
Medica
Moses
Moun
Moun
Newp
Odess
Okan

Berkeley Springs
Bluefield
Buckhannon
Charles Town
Charleston
Clarksburg
Clay
Elkins
Fairmont
Fayetteville
Franklin
Grafton
Grantsville
Harrisville
Hinton
Holden
Huntington
Hurricane
Keyser
Kingwood
Lakin
Lewisburg
Logan
Madison
Man
Mannington
Marlinton
Martinsburg
Montgomery
Moorefield
Morgantown
Moundsville
New Martinsville
Parkersburg
Parsons
Petersburg

Philippi
Pineville
Point Pleasant
Princeton
Ravenswood
Sistersville
Spencer
Sprigg
Triadelphia
Union
Wayne
Webster Springs
Weirton
Welch
West Hamlin
Weston
Wheeling
Williamson

Wisconsin

Adams
Alma
Antigo
Appleton
Arcadia
Arkansas
Ashland
Baraboo
Beloit
Black River Falls
Brookfield
Burlington
Centuria
Chippewa Falls
Clintonville

Cochrane
Cumberland
Dousman
Eau Claire
Elkhorn
Ellsworth
Elm Grove
Elmwood
Fond Du Lac
Friendship
Green Bay
Independence
Janesville
Jefferson
Juneau
Kenosha
Keshena
La Crosse
Ladysmith
Lancaster
Madison
Manawa
Manitowoc
Marinette
Marshfield
Mauston
Medford
Menomonee Falls
Menomonie
Merrill
Milwaukee
Mondovi
Monroe
Montello
Neenah
Neillsville

New London
New Richmond
Niagara
Oconomowoc
Oshkosh
Owen
Plymouth
Port Washington
Portage
Prairie Du Chien
Prairie Du Sac
Prescott
Racine
Reedsburg
Reedsville
Rhinelander
Richland Center
Shawano
Sheboygan
Sheboygan Falls
Siren
Sparta
Stevens Point
Stoughton
Superior
Tomah
Viroqua
Waukesha
Waupaca
Waupun
Wausau
Wauwatosa
West Bend
West Salem
Whitehall
Winnebago

Wisconsin Rapids
Wittenburg

Wyoming

Afton
Buffalo
Casper
Cheyenne
Cody
Douglas
Dubois
Evanston
Gillette
Hulett
Jackson
Jeffrey City
Kemmerer
Lander
Laramie
Newcastle
Pinedale
Rawlins
Riverton
Rock Springs
Sheridan
Sundance
Torrington
Upton
Wheatland

Guam

Agana

Puerto Rico

Aguadilla
Aibonito
Arecibo
Bayamon
Caguas
Canovanas
Carolina
Fajardo
Hato Rey
Humacao
Las Piedras
Manati
Maunabo
Mayaguez
Naguabo
Ponce
Rio Grande
San Juan
Vieques
Yabucoa

Virgin Islands

St. Thomas

VOLUNTARY MENTAL HEALTH ASSOCIATIONS

National Association

Mental Health Association
National Headquarters
1800 North Kent St.
Arlington, Va. 22209

Affiliated Divisions

Mental Health Association in
Alabama
901 18th St., South
Birmingham, Ala. 35205

Arizona Association for Mental
Health
341 West McDowell Road
Phoenix, Ariz. 85003

The Arkansas Association for
Mental Health
424 East Sixth St.
Little Rock, Ark. 72202

California Association for
Mental Health
901 H. St., Suite 212
Sacramento, Calif. 95814

Mental Health Association of
Colorado
1001 Jasmine
Denver, Colo. 80220

Mental Health Association of
Connecticut
56 Arbor St.
Hartford, Conn. 06106

Mental Health Association of Delaware
1813 North Franklin St.
Wilmington, Del. 19802

District of Columbia Mental Health Association
2101 16th St., N.W.
Washington, D.C. 20008

Mental Health Association of Florida
Suite 207, Myrick Bldg.
132 East Colonial Dr.
Orlando, Fla. 32801

The Georgia Association for Mental Health
85 Merritts Ave., N.E.
Atlanta, Ga. 30308

The Mental Health Association of Hawaii
200 N. Vineyard, Room 101
Honolulu, Hawaii 96817

Idaho Mental Health Association
3105½ State St.
Boise, Idaho 83703

Illinois Association for Mental Health
103 North Fifth St., Room 304
Springfield, Ill. 62701

The Mental Health Association in Indiana
1433 N. Meridian St.
Indianapolis, Ind. 46202

The Iowa Association for Mental Health
315 East Fifth St.
Des Moines, Iowa 50309

Kansas Association for Mental Health
1205 Harrison
Topeka, Kans. 66612

The Kentucky Association for Mental Health
Suite 104, 310 West Liberty St.
Louisville, Ky. 40202

The Louisiana Association for Mental Health
1528 Jackson Ave.
New Orleans, La. 70130

Maryland Association for Mental Health
325 East 25th St.
Baltimore, Md. 21218

The Massachusetts Association for Mental Health
38 Chauncy St., Room 801
Boston, Mass. 02111

Michigan Society for Mental Health
27208 Southfield Road
Lathrup Village, Mich. 48075

Minnesota Association for Mental Health
4510 W. 77th St.
Minneapolis, Minn. 55435

Mississippi Association for Mental Health
P. O. Box 5041
Jackson, Miss. 39216

Missouri Association for Mental Health
411 Madison St.
Jefferson City, Mo. 65101

Mental Health Association of Montana
201 S. Last Chance Gulch
Helena, Mont. 69501

Nebraska Association for Mental Health
Lincoln Benefit Life Bldg., Suite 320
134 South 13th St.
Lincoln, Nebr. 68508

New Jersey Association for Mental Health
60 South Fullerton Ave.
Montclair, N.J. 07042

New York State Association for Mental Health
250 West 57th St., Room 1425
New York, N.Y. 10019

North Carolina Mental Health Association
3701 National Dr., Suite 222
Raleigh, N.C. 27612

North Dakota Mental Health Association
P. O. Box 160
Bismarck, N. Dak. 58501

Ohio Association for Mental Health
50 West Broad St., Suite 713
Columbus, Ohio 43215

The Oklahoma Mental Health Association
3113 Classen Blvd.
Oklahoma City, Okla. 73118

Mental Health Association of Oregon
718 W. Burnside St., Room 301
Portland, Oreg. 97209

Pennsylvania Mental Health Association
1207 Chestnut St.
Philadelphia, Pa. 19107

Rhode Island Association for Mental Health
333 Grotto Ave.
Providence, R.I. 02906

South Carolina Mental Health Association
1823 Gadsden St.
Columbia, S.C. 29201

South Dakota Mental Health Association
101½ S. Pierre St., Box 355
Pierre, S. Dak. 57501

*Tennessee Mental Health
    Association*
1717 West End Ave., Suite 421
Nashville, Tenn. 37203

*The Texas Association for
    Mental Health*
103 Lantern Lane
Austin, Tex. 78731

Utah Association for Mental Health
1370 South West Temple
Salt Lake City, Utah 84115

*Virginia Association for
    Mental Health*
1806 Chantilly St., Suite 203
Richmond, Va. 23230

*The West Virginia Association
    for Mental Health*
702½ Lee St.
Charleston, W. Va. 25301

*Wisconsin Association for
    Mental Health*
P. O. Box 1486
Madison, Wis. 53701

Appendix ▐▐▐

STATE
MENTAL HEALTH
AUTHORITIES

Alabama

*State Department of Mental
   Health*
502 Washington Ave.
Montgomery, Ala. 36104
(202) 265-2301

Alaska

*Division of Mental Health
Department of Health and
   Social Services*
Pouch H-04
Juneau, Alaska 99801
(907) 465-3368

Arizona

*Division of Behavioral
   Health Services
Department of Health Services*
2500 E. Van Buren St.
Phoenix, Ariz. 85008
(602) 271-3438

Arkansas

*Division of Mental Health Services
Department of Human Services*
4313 West Markham St.
Little Rock, Ark. 72201
(501) 664-4500

California

Treatment Services Division
State Department of Health
744 P St.
Sacramento, Calif. 95814
(916) 445-1605

Colorado

Division of Mental Health
Department of Institutions
4150 South Lowell Blvd.
Denver, Colo. 80236
(303) 761-0220 X402

Connecticut

Department of Mental Health
90 Washington St.
Hartford, Conn. 06115
(203) 566-3650

Delaware

Division of Mental Health
Department of Health and
*   Social Services*
Governor Bacon Health Center
Delaware City, Del. 19706
(302) 834-9201

District of Columbia

Mental Health Administration
Department of Human Resources

1875 Connecticut Ave., N.W.
Washington, D.C. 20009
(202) 629-3447

Florida

Mental Health Program Office
Department of Health and
*   Rehabilitative Services*
1323 Winewood Blvd.
Tallahassee, Fla. 32301

Georgia

Division of Mental Health and
*   Mental Retardation*
Department of Human Resources
47 Trinity Ave., S.W.
Room 535, Health Bldg.
Atlanta, Ga. 30334
(404) 656-4908

Hawaii

Mental Health Division
Department of Health
P. O. Box 3378
Honolulu, Hawaii 96801
(808) 548-6335

Idaho

Division of Community
*   Rehabilitation*
Department of Health and
*   Welfare*

700 W. State
STATEHOUSE Mail
Boise, Idaho 83720
(208) 384-3920

Illinois

*State Department of
Mental Health and
Developmental Disabilities*
160 N. LaSalle St., Room 1500
Chicago, Ill. 60601
(312) 793-2730

Indiana

*State Department of
Mental Health*
5 Indiana Square
Indianapolis, Ind. 46204
(317) 633-7570

Iowa

*Division of Mental Health
Resources
Department of Social Services*
Lucas State Office Bldg.
Des Moines, Iowa 50319
(515) 281-5497

Kansas

*Division of Mental Health and
Retardation Services*

*State Department of Social and
Rehabilitation Services*
State Office Bldg.
Topeka, Kans. 66612
(913) 296-3774

Kentucky

*Bureau of Health Services
Department for Human Resources*
275 E. Main St.
Frankfort, Ky. 40601
(502) 465-3970

Louisiana

*Division of Mental Health
State Health and Human
Resources Administration*
P. O. Box 44215
Baton Rouge, La. 70804

Maine

*Bureau of Mental Health
State Department of Mental
Health and Corrections*
411 State Office Bldg.
Augusta, Maine 04330
(207) 289-3161

Maryland

*Mental Hygiene Administration
State Department of Health and
Mental Hygiene*

Herbert R. O'Connor State
   Office Bldg.
201 West Preston St.
Baltimore, Md. 21201
(301) 383-2695

Massachusetts

*State Department of
   Mental Health*
190 Portland St.
Boston, Mass. 02141
(617) 727-5600

Michigan

*State Department of
   Mental Health*
Lewis Cass Bldg.
Lansing, Mich. 48926
(517) 373-3500

Minnesota

*Mental Health Program Division
Department of Public Welfare*
Centennial Office Bldg.
St. Paul, Minn. 55155
(612) 296-2710

Mississippi

*State Department of
   Mental Health*

607 Robert E. Lee Office Bldg.
Jackson, Miss. 39201
(601) 354-6132

Missouri

Department of Mental Health
2002 Missouri Blvd.
Jefferson City, Mo. 65101
(314) 751-3070

Montana

*Mental Health Field Services
   Bureau
State Department of Institutions*
1539-11th Ave.
Helena, Mont. 59601
(406) 449-3965

Nebraska
*Division of Medical Services
Department of Public Institutions*
P. O. Box 94723
Lincoln, Nebr. 68509
(402) 471-2851

Nevada

*Division of Mental Hygiene and
   Mental Retardation*
4600 Kietzke Lane, Suite 108
Reno, Nev. 89502
(702) 784-4071

New Hampshire

Division of Mental Health
Department of Health and Welfare
105 Pleasant St.
Concord, N.H. 03301
(603) 271-2366

North Carolina

Division of Mental Health Services
Department of Human Resources
325 N. Salisbury St.
Raleigh, N.C. 27611
(919) 733-7011

New Jersey

Division of Mental Health
and Hospitals
State Department of Institutions
and Agencies
135 W. Hanover St.
Trenton, N.J. 08625

North Dakota

Mental Health and
Retardation Services
Division of Mental Health
and Retardation
State Department of Health
909 Basin Ave.
Bismarch, N. Dak. 58505
(701) 224-2766

New Mexico

Mental Health Division
State Department of Hospitals
and Institutions
113 Washington St.
Sante Fe, N. Mex. 87501
(505) 988-8951

Ohio

State Department of
Mental Health and
Mental Retardation
30 E. Broad St., 12th floor
Columbus, Ohio 43215
(614) 466-2337

New York

State Department of
Mental Hygiene
44 Holland Ave.
Albany, N.Y. 12229
(518) 474-6575

Oklahoma

State Department of Mental Health
P. O. Box 53277
Capitol Station
Oklahoma City, Okla. 73105
(405) 521-2811

Oregon

Mental Health Division
Department of Human Resources
2575 Bittern St., N.E.
Salem, Oreg. 97310
(503) 378-2671

Pennsylvania

Division of Mental Health
State Department of
Public Welfare
Health and Welfare Bldg.,
    Room 308
Harrisburg, Pa. 17120
(717) 787-6443

Rhode Island

Division of Mental Health
Department of Mental Health,
Retardation, and Hospitals
The Aime J. Forand Bldg.
600 New London Ave.
Cranston, R.I. 02920
(401) 464-3291

South Carolina

State Department of Mental Health
P. O. Box 485
Columbia, S.C. 29202
(803) 758-7701

South Dakota

Division of Mental Health and
Mental Retardation
State Department of Social Services
State Office Bldg., Third floor
Illinois St.
Pierre, S. Dak. 57501
(605) 224-3438

Tennessee

Psychiatric Services Division
State Department of
Mental Health and
Mental Retardation
501 Union Bldg.
Nashville, Tenn. 37219
(615) 741-3348

Texas

State Department of
Mental Health and
Mental Retardation
Capitol Station
P. O. Box 12668
Austin, Tex. 78711
(512) 454-3761

Utah

Division of Mental Health
Department of Social Services

554 South Third East
Salt Lake City, Utah 84111
(801) 533-5783

Charleston, W. Va. 25305
(304) 348-3211

Wisconsin

Vermont

Division of Mental Hygiene
State Department of Health and
Social Services
State Office Bldg., Room 534
1 West Wilson St.
Madison, Wis. 53702
(608) 266-2701

State Department of Mental Health
Agency of Human Services
79 River St.
Montpelier, Vt. 05602
(802) 828-2481

Virginia

State Department of
Mental Health and
Mental Retardation
P. O. Box 1797
Richmond, Va. 23214
(804) 786-3921

Wyoming

Mental Health and Mental
Retardation Services
Division of Health and
Medical Services
The Hathaway Bldg.
2300 Capitol Ave.
Cheyenne, Wyo. 82002
(307) 777-7351

Washington

Bureau of Mental Health
Department of Social and
Health Services
Mail Stop 422
Olympia, Wash. 98504

American Samoa

Mental Health
Department of Medical Services
LBJ Tropical Medical Center
Pago Pago, Tutuila
American Samoa 96799

West Virginia

State Department of Mental Health
State Capitol Bldg.

Guam

Community Mental Health Center
Division of Mental Health
Guam Memorial Hospital
P. O. Box AX
Agana, Guam 96910

Trust Territory

Mental Health Division
Department of Health Services
Office of the High Commissioner
Trust Territory of the
    Pacific Islands
Saipan, Mariana Islands 96950

Puerto Rico

Division of Mental Health
Department of Health
G.P.O. Box 61
San Juan, P.R. 00936
(809) 767-9303

Virgin Islands

Division of Mental Health
Department of Health
P. O. Box 1442
St. Thomas, V.I. 00801
(809) 773-1992

FEDERAL MENTAL HEALTH AND MENTAL HEALTH-RELATED INFORMATION SOURCES

Child Abuse:

National Center on Child Abuse
Office of Child Development
P. O. Box 1182
Washington, D.C. 20013

Child Development:

National Institute of Child Health
and Human Development
National Institutes of Health
Bethesda, Md. 20014

Handicapped:

Office for Handicapped Individuals
200 Independence Ave., S.W.,
Rm. 338D
Washington, D.C. 20201

Learning Disorders:

U.S. Office of Education
400 Maryland Ave., S.W.
Room 4159
Washington, D.C. 20202

Mental Retardation: *President's Committee on Mental*
                                     Retardation
                                     Office of Human Development
                                     200 Independence Ave., S.W.
                                     Room 305F
                                     Washington, D.C. 20201

Neurological
   Impairment: *National Institute of Neurological*
                                     and Communicative Disorders
                                     and Stroke
                                     National Institutes of Health
                                     Bethesda, Md. 20014

NATIONAL AGENCIES LISTED BY SPECIAL PROBLEM CATEGORIES

Autism:

National Society for Autistic Children
Information and Referral Service
306 31st St.
Huntington, W. Va. 25702

Child Abuse:

National Committee for the
Prevention of Child Abuse
111 East Wacker Dr.
Room 510
Chicago, Ill. 60601

Child Development:

Day Care and Child Development
Council of America
622 14th St., N.W.
Washington, D.C. 20005

Epilepsy:

Epilepsy Foundation of America
1828 L St., N.W.
Washington, D.C. 20036

Learning Disorders: *Council for Exceptional Children*
                                   1920 Association Dr.
                                   Reston, Va. 22091

Marriage and Family: *American Association of Marriage*
                                   and Family Counselors
                                   225 Yale Ave.
                                   Claremont, Calif. 91711

Mental Retardation: *American Association of*
                                   Mental Deficiency
                                   5201 Connecticut Ave., N.W.
                                   Washington, D.C. 20015

                                   National Association for
                                   Retarded Citizens
                                   2709 Ave. E, East
                                   Arlington, Tex. 76011

Citizens Group for
 Neurological Impairment: *National Committee for Research in*
                                   Neurological and Communicative
                                   Disorders
                                   927 National Press Bldg.
                                   Washington, D.C. 20045

SOME REMEDIAL PROGRAMS FOR SPECIFIC LEARNING DISABILITIES

PERCEPTION

1. The Frostig program for the Development of Visual Perception (Frostig & Horne, 1964)
2. Fairbanks-Robinson Program, Level 1 and Level 2 (Fairbanks & Robinson, 1967)
3. Fitzhugh Plus Program (Fitzhugh & Fitzhugh, 1966)
4. Ruth Chever Program 1 (Chever, 1972)

MOTOR ACTIVITY

1. Dubnoff School Program 1 — Level 2 (Dubnoff, Chambers & Schaffer, 1969)
2. A Guide to Movement Exploration (Hackett & Jensen, 1966)

3. Pathway School Program (Getman, 1969)
4. Vanguard School Program (Robinson & Schmitt, 1970)

SPOKEN LANGUAGE

1. Peabody Language Development Kits (Dun & Smith, 1965, 1966, 1967; Dunn, Horton, & Smith, 1968)
2. DISTAP Language 1 (Engelmann, 1969)
3. The MWM Program for Developing Language Abilities (Minskoff, Wireman, & Minshoff, 1973)
4. Wilson Initial Syntax Program (Wilson, 1972)
5. Efi Special Language Program (1969)

SPELLING

1. Spelling (Buchanan, 1967)
2. Type It (Duffy, 1973)
3. A Spelling Workbook Series (Plunkett & Peck, 1960; Plunkett, 1960; Plunkett, 1961)

ARITHMETIC

1. Cuisenaire Rods (Davidson, 1969)
2. Structural Arithmetic (Stern, Stern, & Gould, 1952)
3. Programmed Math Series One (Sullivan Associates, 1968)
4. Distar Arithmetic (Engelmann & Carnine, 1969)
5. Merrill Mathematics Skilltapes (Spanger, 1969)

6. Mathematics for
   Individual
   Achievement
   (Denholm, et al.,
   1974)

READING

General Approaches

1. Basal Reading
   Series
2. Language
   Experience
3. Programmed
   Reading
4. Linguistics
5. Phonics
6. New Alphabets
7. Multisensory

INDEX